ENTREPRENEURSHIP IN SUPPRESSED MARKETS

PRIVATE-SECTOR EXPERIENCE IN CHINA

DING LU

GARLAND PUBLISHING, INC.
NEW YORK & LONDON / 1994

Library of Congress Cataloging-in-Publication Data

Lu, Ding, 1957–
    Entrepreneurship in suppressed markets : private-sector experience
in China / Ding Lu.
        p.   cm. — (Garland studies in entrepreneurship)
    Includes bibliographical references and index.
    ISBN 0–8153–1643–7
    1. Small business—China.   2. Small business—Government policy—
China.   3. China—Economic policy—1976–   I. Title. II. Series.
HD2346.C6L8   1994
338.6'42'0951—dc20   93–49426
                                                                                    CIP

Printed on acid-free, 250-year-life paper
Manufactured in the United States of America

GARLAND STUDIES IN ENTREPRENEURSHIP

edited by

STUART BRUCHEY
UNIVERSITY OF MAINE

A GARLAND SERIES

to my homeland

CONTENTS

LIST OF TABLES

LIST OF FIGURES

List of Figures

PREFACE

Entrepreneurship plays a crucial role in economic development. The literature of entrepreneurship embodies two major issues. One is the issue of identification, which concerns the nature and role of entrepreneurs; the other is the issue of significance, which deals with the socioeconomic environment of entrepreneurial activity. Most studies have focused on the positive potentials of entrepreneurship and presumed that all entrepreneurial activities are productive. Little academic efforts have been attempted to classify different types of entrepreneurial activities and to examine the institutional settings that nurture them. A rarely investigated area is the complicated interaction between entrepreneurial behavior and the changes of economic institutions.

This book offers a broad perspective by showing that both the welfare effects of entrepreneurial activity and the supply of entrepreneurship are highly influenced by institutional settings. The supply of entrepreneurship is more a problem of quality and direction rather than one of volume and intensity. Economic development stagnates when institutional settings channel society's entrepreneurial capacity to less productive uses. In particular, the political power that suppresses market operation may create contrived benefits accompanied by persistent disequilibria. The entrepreneurial action devised to secure access to these benefits may generate competition that wastes economic resources.

This observation suggests that the relationship between entrepreneurial behavior and its institutional constraints can be best observed and analyzed in economic systems where the market forces are suppressed by administrative intervention and control. The private-sector experience in the People's Republic of China serves as a case exceptionally good for the examination of the relationship. From 1949 to 1990 China's private sector underwent drastic institutional changes. It diminished during the 1950s when China was transformed from a market economy to a centrally-planned command economy. It was then severely suppressed and almost totally eliminated during the Mao era when the country's economy suffered political instability. Later in the 1980s the private sector revived as an overall reform transformed the system back toward a market economy. This book probes the causes and social impact of waxing and waning of China's private entrepreneurship. The results confirm that, during the period examined, the role of entrepreneurship was sensitive to the institutional restrictions imposed on the private sector. It is also found that private entrepreneurs played a pivotal role in a series of institutional innovations during the economic reform of the 1980s. In China's transitional economic system, there have emerged plenty of rent-seeking opportunities for unproductive entrepreneurship. The experience has important implications on the future path of China's economic development.

ACKNOWLEDGMENTS

This book, a revised version of my Ph.D. dissertation, would not have been completed without the help and support of a number of people. First of all, I would like to express my gratitude and appreciation to the members of my dissertation committee, Professor John C. Panzar, Professor Morton I. Kamien, and Professor Michael A. Marrese. Their encouragement, advice, and insightful comments helped me throughout my work on the research. I especially owe my thanks to Professor Marrese, the Chairperson of the Dissertation Committee, for his academic guidance, friendly suggestions, and valuable time spent with me.

I thank Garland Publishing Inc. for offering me this opportunity to be a part of its series of studies on entrepreneurship. My special gratitude goes to Dr. Stuart Bruchey, General Editor of the series, for recommending the publication of this book. I would also express my appreciation of Mr. Robert McKenzie's coordination that has facilitated the book's publication.

I gratefully acknowledge the financial supports that I received from Pepsi Cola Foundation and Northwestern University for my Ph.D. program. I benefitted from discussion with participants of the Twilight Zone Seminar at Department of Economics of Northwestern University and 1990 Summer Workshop on Soviet Union and East European Economics sponsored by Social Science Research Council. My friends, Renze Zhang and Hong Chen, at China Statistical Information and Consultancy Service Center of the University of Illinois at Chicago provided valuable assistance in my search for statistical data.

Also, many thanks should go to my fellow graduate colleagues, Carolyn Berry, Michael Chwe, Victor Li, Mark Witte, Herbert Wong and others, for their encouragement, friendship, and time spent on helping me proofread the manuscripts. I would like to extend my thanks to Karen Bandusch, Paula Nielsen, and Jackie Olsen for their professional support in computer work. I greatly appreciate Tamila Ghodsi's editorial assistance.

Acknowledgments

Finally, but not least, I wish to express my hearty thanks to my family. My parents and parents-in-law have always been supportive to my academic pursuit. To my two children, Stephanie and Daniel, I owe an apology for whatever they were deprived of when I was engrossed in writing this book. Stephanie was several months old when I finished the work of my Ph.D. dissertation in 1991 while Daniel was only a few weeks old when I printed the completed manuscript of this book. I wish in future the two kids would find this book interesting. I am especially grateful to my wife, Qing, for her love, support, understanding and patience during my years at Northwestern University and the period I revised the manuscript for publication.

Entrepreneurship in
Suppressed Markets

CHAPTER 1

INTRODUCTION

1.1 Objectives of the Study

Entrepreneurship is the source of economic vitality. Entrepreneurs create business opportunities, establish firms, organize production, and improve resource allocation by their innovative, risk-taking, and opportunity-seeking activities. Countries, poor or wealthy, need entrepreneurial spirit to support economic growth, sharpen their competitive edge, and raise productivity.

The importance of entrepreneurship to economic development cannot be over-emphasized. This, however, should not lead to a naive belief that entrepreneurship per se would always be a blessing for society regardless the institutional environment. Entrepreneurial activity is purely profit-oriented. Entrepreneurs can provide "bads" as well as goods to society. In a well functioning market economy, entrepreneurs are the people who engineer a nation's productivity growth. In certain circumstances, however, entrepreneurs could be the producers who exploit consumers upon asymmetric information and market power. It is also possible for entrepreneurs to be involved in illegal activities such as political scandals or even organized crimes. The role of entrepreneurship varies with differing institutional settings. The literature of entrepreneurship nevertheless offers little investigation on this complicated interaction between the welfare effects of entrepreneurial behavior and the institutional environment.

This observation has motivated this research. It aims to contribute to the literature by introducing a broad perspective on the role of entrepreneurship. By reviewing the private sector experience in the People's Republic of China, this research also presents an empirical study to examine the impact of institutional changes on entrepreneurial behavior.

3

1.2 The Literature of Entrepreneurship

Most studies in the literature about entrepreneurship focus on two major issues. One is the issue of identification, which concerns the nature and role of entrepreneurs; the other is the issue of significance, which deals with the socioeconomic environment of entrepreneurial activity.

Researchers of the first issue try to answer the question, "Who is an entrepreneur?" For a long time, social scientists' research on the issue had much in common with "Heffalump hunting," an analogy made by P. Kilby.[1] To researchers in the field, entrepreneurship was like the awesome animal known as the "Heffalump" in the Winnie-the-Pooh stories, which had been described in different ways but never captured.

Thanks to weighty attention paid to entrepreneurship during the last two decades, the nature of entrepreneurship is no longer that mysterious. Researchers following the "trait approach" have revealed different aspects of entrepreneurs' traits and personality characteristics, while those following the "behavioral approach" have identified the dynamic role and behavior of entrepreneurs in socioeconomic development.[2] Both types of studies have enriched our knowledge of the phenomenon.

The definition of the nature and role of entrepreneurs leads to the second issue of the literature: what socioeconomic environment is necessary to support the growth of entrepreneurship? Differing views on this subject and the division of labor in research have divided economists and non-economist social scientists in their answers to the question. Most economists regard entrepreneurship primarily as a dependent variable in economic development, a response to the opportunities emerging in a given situation. In contrast, non-economist social scientists, particularly sociologists, psychologists, and anthropologists, usually view entrepreneurship as a significant and independent variable in the economic process, which is mainly decided by non-economic factors. They argue that the supply of entrepreneurship is exogenously given by non-economic social background and therefore cannot be substantially affected by changes in economic incentives.[3]

Relatively little work has been done to identify different types of entrepreneurial activities and their social welfare effects. Studies on both issues in the literature treat the nature and role of entrepreneurship with little regard to its welfare effects. In spite of their differing views, most social scientists, including economists, have taken the potential benefits of the supply of entrepreneurship as given. The quality and direction of entrepreneurial activity are usually not explicitly studied.

Some writers have noticed that entrepreneurial activity is the pursuit of pure profit and does not automatically guarantee improvement of social welfare; its welfare effects are therefore sensitive to institutional settings.[4] Buchanan, Tollison, and Tullock,[5] Bhagwati,[6] and others have developed the literature about rent-seeking, an important type of unproductive and socially-wasteful business activity. More recently, Baumol provided abundant historical evidence to show that the vigor of economic growth is greatly affected by the way society allocates its entrepreneurial resources.[7] He argued that uses of entrepreneurial efforts may be productive, unproductive, and even destructive, depending on the institutional structures that specify the relative payoffs to different entrepreneurial activities.

In recent years, economists have conducted some studies on the allocation of limited managerial attention among productive uses at the firm level. Radner and Rothschild[8] and Winter[9] modeled the cost minimizing allocation of a manager's effort among projects. Holmstrom and Milgrom [10] studied the optimal contracts to allocate agents' attention among multiple tasks under incomplete information. Gifford and Wilson[11] delineated the allocation of entrepreneurial attention between current projects and innovative projects. A few economists have examined economy-wide resource allocation between productive uses and unproductive, rent-seeking uses. Their studies generally assume that rent-seeking business is separated from productive activity. Magee, Brock, and Young[12] presented a model to describe the allocation of labor between rent-seeking and production. Murphy, Shleifer, and Vishny[13] studied the allocation of talented people between a rent-seeking sector and a productive sector.

1.3 Rationale

The review of the literature of entrepreneurship shows that the research in the field has been biased toward the productive aspect of entrepreneurship. Most studies have presumed, implicitly or explicitly, that productive entrepreneurship is the only form of the phenomenon. Little academic efforts have been attempted to classify different types of entrepreneurial activities and to examine the institutional settings that nurtures them.

This study is primarily inspired by the insights of Baumol's comments on entrepreneurship.[14] The excavation of entrepreneurial resources itself cannot guarantee that social welfare will improve. The welfare impact of entrepreneurship as well as the supply of entrepreneurship itself is sensitive to institutional changes. The supply of entrepreneurship is more a problem of quality and direction rather than one of volume and intensity. Ill-structured institutional settings may induce unproductive business practice that wastes scarce resources. Rent-seeking, or contrived surplus seeking, is the most important form of unproductive business activity in modern society. Rent-seeking opportunity mainly comes from the political power that meddles in market operation. Therefore the relationship between entrepreneurial behavior and its institutional constraints can be best observed and analyzed in economic systems where the market forces are suppressed by administrative intervention. This research aims to extend our understanding of entrepreneurship by (a) offering a taxonomy that categorizes different types of entrepreneurial activities according to their welfare effects and interaction with economic institutions; and by (b) analyzing the role of entrepreneurship in markets suppressed by central planning or regulation.

The institutional environment of the private sector in the People's Republic of China may serve as an ideal empirical setting for the examination of the role and nature of entrepreneurship in suppressed markets. China has experienced the waxing and waning of her private sector in an unsteady centrally-planned economy. During the four decades from 1949 to 1990, the government's policy toward the private economy has undergone tremendous changes. In both the periods of Socialist Transformation in the 1950s and Economic Reform in the 1980s, the Chinese economy was undergoing a transition: in the former period, a transition from a market economy to a centrally-planned one; in the latter period, a transition from a centrally-planned one back to a basically market-oriented economy. The Chinese economy in the Mao era was also full of instability due to the wavering of the political pendulum. It is hard to find another economy in the post-war world in which the institutional environment of the private sector has varied so frequently and so drastically as has been the case in China. Therefore, the history of China's private economy provides an exceptionally valuable case for the study of entrepreneurial activities in a sporadically suppressed market.

1.4 Organization of the Study

This book includes eight chapters. The Chapters 2 and 3 lay down the conceptual foundation of the research. Through a literature review of entrepreneurship and rent-seeking activity, Chapter 2 develops a taxonomy as to categorize two major types of entrepreneurial activities: productive, profit-seeking activity, and unproductive, rent-seeking activity. This approach identifies rent-seeking as the basic form of unproductive entrepreneurial activity in modern society. In markets suppressed by government regulation or central planning, disequilibria persist and contrived surpluses or rents result. When entrepreneurial actions are devised to secure access to these contrived benefits, rent-seeking occurs and the resulting unproductive use of resources causes deadweight loss to society.

Chapter 3 analyzes how the role of entrepreneurial activity varies in a suppressed market. When the real prices facing firms and consumers are distorted, the welfare effects of productive entrepreneurship will also be distorted. In the case where the contrived benefits resulting from price distortion become a goal of business, entrepreneurial activity will waste resources when it reacts to the distortion as an equilibrating market force.

The main body of the book, Chapters 4, 5, 6, and 7, explores the role of entrepreneurship in suppressed markets in the context of China's private sector experience. Chapter 4 shows that, when the Chinese government suppressed market forces during the Socialist Transformation (1949 to 1956), the nature of private entrepreneurship drastically changed and the capitalist sector consequently lost its competitive edge and innovative dynamics. Chapter 5 discusses the private-sector experience in the Mao era (1957 to 1978).[15] During this period entrepreneurial activities, in a variety of forms, were highly sensitive to the institutional changes caused by the wavering of official policies. Chapter 6 recounts the revival of the private sector in the post-Mao economic reform (1978 to 1990) and evaluates the active role of private entrepreneurs in initiating a series of institutional innovations. Chapter 7 examines the economic chaos that emerged in the late 1980s. It appears that a major cause of the economic predicament in the period

Entrepreneurship in Suppressed Markets

was the increasing opportunities for rent-seeking provided by the transitional institutions. The last chapter discusses the implications of the institutional features of China's transitional economy on the future development of entrepreneurship.

1.5 Data of the Study

In this study, sources of information regarding China's private sector are mainly (ranked by their importance): (a) Chinese government official publications of statistical data and documents; (b) published articles and books of Chinese government officials, retired officials, and senior consultants; (c) news reports from Chinese official newspapers; (d) established results of Western writers' academic research on Chinese economy and politics; (e) other reports or papers about developments in China. This research makes extensive use of official Chinese statistics. Although in the past Chinese official statistics were notoriously incomplete and rudimentary, serious efforts have been made in recent years by the Chinese statistical organs to improve the quantity as well as quality of Chinese statistical data. For instance, the major Chinese statistical handbook of the 1950s, *Ten Great Years*, contained only 200 pages of tables and publication of all statistics by China virtually ceased between 1960 to 1980.[16] During the 1980s, however, the Chinese government published economic data at an accelerating rate. The official 1986 statistical yearbook, for example, contains over 800 pages of data, each page containing much more data than its 1950s equivalent. In addition, many provincial governments and ministries have published their own statistical data.[17] Assisted by the World Bank and the United Nations, the State Statistical Bureau of China, with more than 60,000 staff nationwide, embarked on a project in the recent years to substantially improve the quality of Chinese statistics by adopting an internationally comparable GNP accounting system.[18] Since 1989, a series of revised English language editions of the official Chinese statistical publications have been compiled by the China Statistical Information and Consultancy Service Center in the United States and published by Praeger Publishers in New York. These publications provide the official Chinese statistical data with improved quality.

A few words are needed to explain source (b). Due to the lack of officially published statistical data before 1980, especially during the period from 1960 to 1980, the information cited in Chapter 4 and 5 relies heavily on the works of some Chinese authors such as Xue Muqiao, Xu Dixin, Yu Guangyuan, and Liu Suinian and Wu Qungan. These writers are/were either senior government officials or consultants.[19] Although in these authors' works, sources of information are usually not provided explicitly, there is no reason to doubt that their accounts are reliably based on official data and their personal experience.[20] Therefore, these works offer the most credible and authoritative published Chinese sources next to official documents. This research gives special attention to the consistency of the data sources. When it is possible, the validity of the data is checked against the findings of other independent researchers.

NOTES

1. Kilby, P., *Entrepreneurship and Economic Development*, New York: Free Press, 1971.

2. Gartner, William B., "'Who is an Entrepreneur?' Is the Wrong Question," *Entrepreneurship Theory and Practice*, 1988, Spring issue.

3. For an account of these competing views, see Wilken, P.H., *Entrepreneurship: a Comparative and Historical Study*, Norwood, NJ: Ables Publishing Corporation, 1979, pp. 2-4, pp. 26-27. Also, see Fairbairn, Te'o I.J., *Island Entrepreneurs*, Honolulu, Hawaii: The East-West Center Books, 1988, pp. 19-22.

4. Hughes, Jonathan R.T., "Entrepreneurship," *Dictionary of Economic History*, Boston: Little Brown, 1980, pp. 214-228. Also, Marrese, Michael. "Entrepreneurship, Liberalization, and Social Tension," *Jahrbuch der Wirtshaft Osteuropas* Vol.14, no.1, 1990, pp. 1-15.

5. Buchanan, J. M., R.D. Tollison and G. Tullock ed., *Toward a Theory of the Rent-Seeking Society*, U.S.A.: Texas A & M University Press, 1980.

6. Bhagwati, J. N., "Directly Unproductive, Profit-seeking (DUP) Activities," *Journal of Political Economy,* Vol.90, no.5, 1982, pp. 988-1002.

7. Baumol, William. "Entrepreneurship: Productive, Unproductive, and Destructive," *Journal of Political Economy.* Vol.98, no.5, pt I, 1990, pp. 893-921.

8. Radner, R. and M. Rothschild, "On Allocation of Effort," *Journal of Economic Theory.* no. 10, 1975, pp. 358-376.

9. Winter, S. G. "The Case for 'Mechanistic' Decision Making," *Organizational Strategy and Change*, J. M. Pennings et al ed. San Francisco: Jossey-Bass Publishers, 1985, pp. 99-113.

10. Holmstrom, B. and P. Milgrom, "Multi-Task Principal/Agent Analysis: Incentive Contracts, Asset Ownership and Job Design," Working Paper #45, Series D, Yale School of Organization and Management, 1990.

11. Gifford, S. E. and C. A. Wilson, "A Model of Optimal Inspection and Repair of an Endogenous Number of Projects," C.V. Starr working paper #90-06, New York University, 1990.

12. Magee, Stephen P., William R. Brock, and Leslie Young, *Black Hole Tariffs and the Endogenous Policy Theory*, Cambridge: Cambridge University Press, 1989.

13. Murphy, Kevin M., Andrei Shleifer, and Robert W. Vishny, "The Allocation of Talent: Implications for Growth," *The Quarterly Journal of Economics*, Vol.106, May 1991, pp. 503-530.

14. Baumol, W. op. cit.

15. Mao's ideology continued to be the guideline of China's policy-making after Mao's death (September 1976) until Mao's selected successor Hua Guofeng was deprived of his power at the end of 1978.

16. State Statistical Bureau of The People's Republic of China (PRC), *Ten Great Years*, Beijing: Foreign Language Press, 1960.

17. According to Perkins, Dwight H., "Reforming China's Economic System," *Journal of Economic Literature*, Vol. 26, June 1988, pp. 601-645.

18. *Renmin Ribao* (People's Daily) [Beijing, China], 25 Jan. 1991, p.1.

19. Xue Muqiao, the director of China's Economic Research Center from the late 1970s to the 1980s, was a senior government official in charge of the policy making of the Socialist Transformation in the 1950s. Liu and Wu "have long been working in various economic departments [of the government]" [Xue Muqiao, "Preface," Liu Suinian and Wu Qungan ed., *China's Socialist Economy—— An Outline History (1949-1984)*, Beijing, China: Beijing Review, 1986, p. 2.] Liu

was appointed the head of Material Department in the late 1980s. [*Renmin Ribao* (People's Daily), 6 July 1990, p. 3.] Xu Dixin, who used to be head of China's Central Industrial and Commercial Administrative Bureau during the 1950s and 1960s, is a well known senior economist in China. Yu Guangyuan, the deputy director of China's Science and Technology Commission in the 1950s and 1960s and a senior researcher in China's National Academy of Social Sciences in the 1980s, was in charge of government economic policy making in the early 1950s and in charge of organization of social science research in most of the 1960s and the 1980s. [Ref: Editorial Committee, *Chung Kung Jen Ming Lu* (Who is Who in the CPC), Taipei, Taiwan: Institute of International Relations, 1967, 1985].

20. *China's Socialist Economy——An Outline History (1949-1984)*, for example, was written by a team of staff of China's Economic Research Center "on the basis of the large quantities of [official] documents and materials they had collected and sifted." [Xue Muqiao, loc. cit.]

CHAPTER 2

THE ROLE OF ENTREPRENEURSHIP

2.1 Introduction

The growth of entrepreneurship, as a key component of socioeconomic development, has been a fascinating topic in social sciences. In economics, entrepreneurial capacity has long been acknowledged as a crucial factor of production. As part of the conceptual foundation of the book, this chapter offers a broad perspective on the role of entrepreneurs. We will establish a taxonomy of different types of entrepreneurial activities based on their socioeconomic functions. The purpose is to synthesize the theoretical results in the existing literature about entrepreneurship. The analysis will advance along the lines of the two major issues in the literature, i.e., identification, which concerns the nature and role of entrepreneurs; and significance, which deals with the socioeconomic environment of entrepreneurial activity.

Section 2.2 starts with a review of the different theories related to entrepreneur identification. Based on earlier theories, we modify the definition of entrepreneurship in an economic sense by the distinction between its two major economic roles: equilibration and innovation. Section 2.3 compares the dividing views of entrepreneurship and discusses their implication on policy making. Section 2.4 further comments on the prevailing presumption of the role of entrepreneurs and suggests the need to identify different types of entrepreneurial activities. Section 2.5 develops such an approach by categorizing entrepreneurial activities according to their socioeconomic functions under different institutional settings.

13

2.2 The Economic Role of Entrepreneurship

There have developed many theories concerning the nature and role of entrepreneurship since the study of the issue was started by scholars of the eighteenth century. After reviewing the works of dozens of writers in the literature, R. Hebert and A. Link summarized concepts of entrepreneurship.[1] An entrepreneur has been described as:

—— a business starter;

—— an industrial leader;

—— an innovator;

—— the person who assumes the risk associated with uncertainty;

—— a supplier of venture capital;

—— a business decision maker;

—— a manager or superintendent;

—— a proprietor of an enterprise;

—— an employer of factors of production;

—— a contractor;

—— a business coordinator;

—— a disequilibrium-gap-filler (an arbitrageur or speculator);

—— the person who allocates resources to alternative uses.

Some of these concepts are preliminary and rough; some are obviously overlapping. Generally, there appear to be two ways to delineate entrepreneurship: the trait approach and the behavioral approach. The research following the "trait approach" mainly deals with the static personality of entrepreneurs. The result of such studies is the identification of some traits and characteristics related to entrepreneurship, or a "psychological profile" of the entrepreneur. It reveals that entrepreneurship is rooted in some particular qualities of human nature, that is, an alertness to opportunities, an ability to quickly take advantage of opportunities, creative imagination, the courage to bear risks, and so forth. However, critics of the trait approach point out that this approach, which concentrates on the personality of entrepreneurs, is not sufficient to provide us with a real understanding of the phenomenon.[2] It is argued that research on the entrepreneur should focus on what the entrepreneur does rather than who the entrepreneur is, because entrepreneurship refers to a type of dynamic social behavior. As many writers have pointed out, the traits and personality characteristics of entrepreneurs are actually potential human capabilities everyone possesses. Whenever those qualities are active in socioeconomic life, the resulting behavior is entrepreneurial.[3] So a more meaningful approach to the issue is to define the dynamic behavior of the entrepreneur.

Many have noticed that the dynamic aspect of entrepreneurship involves a combination of production factors. Therefore, they view entrepreneurship as activity to *organize businesses*. Moreover, to distinguish entrepreneurship from management, which also involves the organization of production, some writers, such as Gartner, define entrepreneurship as activity to *start new businesses or create new organizations*.[4] This behavioral definition of entrepreneurship, however, does not expose some important features of entrepreneurial behavior, such as disequilibrium-gap-filling, innovation, and risk-taking, all of which may not necessarily involve starting a new firm. An alternative way to define entrepreneurship and distinguish it from management is to emphasize the changes brought to production routines by entrepreneurial activities.[5] Entrepreneurship must involve something novel to the production process and business activity.

Then what types of changes are initiated by entrepreneurs? Hebert and Link summarize different views on the role of entrepreneurship as four types of theories.[6] Pure Uncertainty theories stress uncertainty as the chief problem handled by the entrepreneur, put forward by R. Cantillon, F. Knight, L. Mises, and others.[7] Pure Innovation theories, developed by G. Schmöller, M. Weber, J. Schumpeter and others, stress innovation instead of uncertainty.[8] Uncertainty and Ability /Innovation theories, backed by J. Bentham, J. M. von Thünen, and A. H. Cole, treat entrepreneurship as a combination of risk bearing and either innovation or some special ability.[9] Another group of economists like J. B. Clark, I. Kirzner and T. W. Schultz present the Perception and Adjustment theories that emphasize the perception of and adjustment to disequilibria.[10] In synthesizing these various perspectives, Hebert and Link pointed out that all these theories have centered either on uncertainty, innovation, or on some combination of the two. They recognize that uncertainty is a consequence of change whereas innovation is primarily a cause of change.[11]

Uncertainty involves imperfect information about changes. Because of imperfect information, inefficiency exists everywhere. Leibenstein's X-efficiency theory describes the essential characteristics of business environment as a world of inefficiency.[12] Hayek visualizes a business world in which there is continuous process of discovery related to technological changes and market disequilibria.[13] Based on similar views, Kirzner depicts the world as one characterized by numerous disequilibria, most of which are ignored by non-entrepreneurs.[14] Therefore, he defines entrepreneurship as alertness to disequilibria and the action to exploit the associated arbitrage opportunities. For Kirzner, this should be the only possible nature of entrepreneurial activity. In his theory, even the invention of a "revolutionarily" new machine is an equilibrating process, in the sense that it eliminates the disequilibria between the given knowledge of technology and its application in production. Among the theorists who share similar views is M. Casson, who defines the role of the entrepreneur as a coordinator of economic activities.[15]

At the other extreme, J. Schumpeter's view was of a world essentially in general equilibrium with a state of "circular flow," which would be disturbed and intruded upon by entrepreneurs with their innovations.[16] A Schumpeterian innovation encompasses introduction of new products and new methods of production, opening new markets, exploiting new sources of raw materials and finding new ways to organize an industry. It introduces new production functions, triggers the process of "creative-destruction," and produces disequilibrating changes.

These two extreme points of view are not as contradictory as they seem to be. In a world of incomplete information, the market status quo is an equilibrium in the eyes of non-entrepreneurs. The non-entrepreneurs would consider any innovation to the status quo to be a disequilibrating force, whereas the entrepreneurs who possess superior information could perceive the hidden disequilibria and take advantage of them. They view the market as initially in a disequilibrium state and their own action as equilibrating. Entrepreneurs and non-entrepreneurs thus hold different views about the state of the market and entrepreneurial activity ex ante.

There is, however, another interpretation in which entrepreneurs do not necessarily possess superior information and they themselves are equally uncertain about the consequences of their actions. Both entrepreneurs and non-entrepreneurs may have the same evaluation of the state of the market here. Both ex ante and ex post, they may consider the innovation to be a disturbance to the status quo, or a disequilibrating change. Entrepreneurs simply possess some different perceptions or attitude toward the risk and uncertainty the innovation involves. In the history of technology development, the inventor of a new gadget may not be the best-informed scientist who possesses information superior to that of others, but the one who has imagination, courage (a special attitude to risk), and good luck.

Therefore, theoretically speaking, entrepreneurial activities can be distinguished as equilibrating and disequilibrating (innovative), according to the ex ante and ex post views of entrepreneurs and non-entrepreneurs. As defined by J. Hughes, "entrepreneurial activity is the pursuit of pure profit through the exploitation of existing disequilibria or through the creation of disequilibria by the introduction of new products, methods, or techniques into the stream of economic life."[17] Equilibrating entrepreneurial activity alters the accepted allocation of resources as a reaction to disequilibrium. If the entrepreneur is the person who perceives the disequilibrium and reacts faster than other people to fill the gaps, his activity is equilibrating. On the other hand, innovative entrepreneurial activity is a real shock to the existing equilibrium for both the entrepreneurs and non-entrepreneurs. The innovative entrepreneur does not necessarily possess information superior to that of other people, but simply has the imagination and the courage. The innovative activity can be technological, organizational, or even institutional, as long as it introduces new production functions.[18]

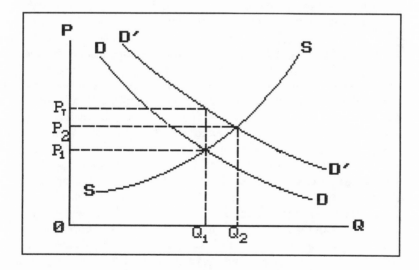

Figure 2.1 Equilibrating Entrepreneurial Activity

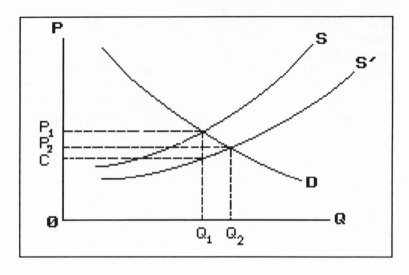

Figure 2.2 Disequilibrating Entrepreneurial Activity

These two categories of entrepreneurial activity can be illustrated in a simple partial equilibrium context. Consider a competitive market where adjustment to disequilibrium situations takes time. In Figure 2.1, when the market supply is Q_1 and price is at P_1, non-entrepreneurs do not see any opportunity for abnormal profits, thinking that the market has reached a stable equilibrium where demand curve D intersects supply curve S. However, the entrepreneurs who possess superior information anticipate that the demand will soon shift to D', and when that happens, a temporary monopolistic price (P_T) can be charged and abnormal profits can be earned before the quantity supplied increases to Q_2. As demand shifts, the entrepreneurs are faster than others to increase the quantity supplied, and enjoy the windfall abnormal profits. Their activity increases the quantity supplied, dissipates the temporary abnormal profits, and drives the market to a new equilibrium (where price is P_2 and quantity is Q_2). This entrepreneurial activity is equilibrating. In Figure 2.2, when the market equilibrium price P_1 and quantity Q_1 are determined by the intersection of the supply curve S and demand curve D, the entrepreneurs and non-entrepreneurs share the same perception of the market equilibrium. By adopting a new combination of productive factors or a new production function, innovative entrepreneurs lower their marginal production cost to C and enjoy (temporary) abnormal profits (P_1 - C) because of the disequilibrium they have created. When the innovation prevails in the industry, the supply curve shifts out to S'. Here the entrepreneurial activity is disequilibrating.

An extreme case of disequilibrating entrepreneurial activity is market creation, which is illustrated in Figure 2.3 and 2.4. In Figure 2.3, before entrepreneurs' innovation occurs, production cost is so high such that the supply curve S_1 does not intersect the demand curve D and therefore the market does not exist. In other words, suppliers are not willing to sell at any price that consumers are willing to pay. After the innovation, however, the supply curve shifts out so that S_2 intersects the demand curve and the market is created. Figure 2.4 shows how entrepreneurs may "open" a market by influencing consumers' preferences. Originally, market demand is so low that consumers cannot afford any price suppliers are willing to sell. After entrepreneurs use marketing techniques to persuade consumers, the market demand is pushed up to D_2, and the market is "opened."

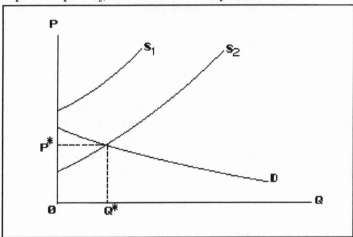

Figure 2.3   Market Creation (Supply Side)

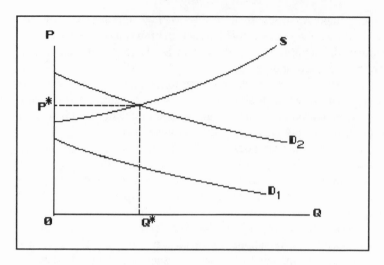

Figure 2.4   Market Creation (Demand Side)

This classification of the roles of entrepreneurial activity defines entrepreneurship purely from its effects on market equilibria, therefore, it does not involve any presumed value judgement of such activity. Equilibrating or disequilibrating, the entrepreneurial activity may or may not improve general social welfare. Without a description of more specific institutional settings, we cannot comment on the welfare effects of the entrepreneurial activity. The merit of a purely descriptive definition of entrepreneurship can be better understood by the discussion of the controversial "economist's view" of the supply of entrepreneurship.

2.3 Dividing Views of Entrepreneurship

For decades, main stream economists have received criticism for their alleged ignorance and inadequate study of entrepreneurial behavior. A major critique points to its "excessively narrow definition of the entrepreneurial function."[19] Some critics claim that economists have a problem of "failure to specify entrepreneurship as a separate factor input."[20] According to Kilby, the economists' definition of entrepreneurship is based on the unrealistic assumptions of a high degree of factor mobility, homogeneity of inputs and outputs, complete and symmetric information, and divisibility of all goods.[21] Once these assumptions are relaxed, the extraordinary qualities required of the entrepreneur and the possibility of their limited supply becomes apparent.

The weight of entrepreneurship in economic analysis also invites criticism. For many years static equilibrium analysis has been the major approach of economic research. Kirzner criticizes the assumption of general equilibrium theory that all market participants are price-takers under perfect competition.[22] By assuming the function of a Walrasian Auctioneer, economists exclude the role of the entrepreneur from the equilibrating process and cultivate the illusion of instant adjustment of the market process. They have thus fallen into the trap of taking the equilibrating forces for granted and assuming no entrepreneurial work remains to be done. According to Hayek, the assumption of market equilibrium in neoclassical economic analysis is equivalent to a postulate of full information.[23] Neoclassical economic analysis usually simplifies the market process down to some optimizing calculation subject to some known constraints, leaving little room for novel ventures. As Kirzner shows, the incentive to make choices between known opportunities is quite different from the incentive to be alert to a potential opportunity.[24] An unparalleled advantage of the market economy is its ability to provide incentives for innovative entrepreneurship. Neoclassical economists unfortunately failed to model this outstanding feature for a long time.

To some extent, critiques directed at analytic techniques in economics have become a passé in the recent years. Recent developments in the fields of information economics, industrial organization, innovation, and the theory of firm have provided powerful analytical tools for the study of optimization problems under incomplete information and uncertainty. Today's economists are no longer constrained to static analyses of equilibrium outcomes without understanding the underlying dynamic process. Great progress has been made to delineate entrepreneurial activities in the "standard" language of economics.[25]

In spite of these developments, the many critiques pointing to economists' general attitude toward entrepreneurship still reflect the fundamental differences in the viewpoints of (mainstream) economists and other social scientists on the issue. In the following discussion, we will refer to mainstream economists' view of the supply of entrepreneurship as the "economist's view," and the arguments against the "economist's view" as the "non-economist's view." According to the "economist's view," entrepreneurship is mainly a dependent variable in socioeconomic development. The intensity of entrepreneurial activities is sensitive to economic factors such as the abundance of profit-seeking opportunities. These economic factors are defined by Wilken as the "opportunity conditions" of the supply of entrepreneurship.[26] Economic growth and the supply of entrepreneurship are correlated with each other because of their dependence on such conditions. As proper incentives are provided in an economy, the supply of entrepreneurial services expands correspondingly.[27] Therefore, economists generally do not believe that an inadequate supply of entrepreneurship should be a fundamental exogenous obstacle to economic growth. In other words, the opportunity conditions or economic incentives are the major significant factors, determining both the supply of entrepreneurship and the rate of economic growth.

The "non-economist's view" holds that the factors determining the supply of entrepreneurship are given exogenously by certain cultural, ethic, and sociological backgrounds. Therefore, a change in the economic incentive system cannot substantially affect the supply of entrepreneurship. The supply of entrepreneurship affects the rate of economic growth independently of other growth-related economic factors. When the supply of entrepreneurship is not sensitive to economic incentives, the lack of entrepreneurial resources may remain to be a serious obstacle to economic development no matter whether the proper economic incentives are provided. Therefore, non-economic factors are significant for the supply of entrepreneurship and economic growth.

One of the attempts to test the validity of these competing views was conducted by Wilken, who distinguished what he called the definitional and causal significance of entrepreneurship.[28] Definitional significance, which is accepted by both economists and non-economists, refers to the initiating activities of human actors in economic life. Causal significance, which is mainly accepted by non-economist social scientists, emphasizes entrepreneurship's independent additive influence on economic growth. To examine the existence of causal significance, Wilken studied the industrialization history of six western countries and compared the rates of industrial growth and the favorableness of the economic opportunity conditions for entrepreneurship. He expected that, if the rate of industrial growth significantly deviated from the change of favorableness of the opportunity conditions in a society, the phenomenon would indicate that economic growth depends on something other than economic opportunity conditions. This would then support the argument that entrepreneurship has an independent "causal" effect on economic growth. Contrarily, a proportionate relation between the rate of industrial growth and the favorableness of economic opportunity conditions would suggest that entrepreneurship should have little causal significance, being determined by more basic "causes"(conditions) of economic growth. Wilken's study supports the conjecture that entrepreneurship is of little causal significance in the industrial transition of these societies. His study also shows that both economic and non-economic factors constitute necessary conditions for the emergence of entrepreneurship.

Recent research on entrepreneurship in economic development also appears to support the "economists'" conjecture. It used to be widely believed among social scientists that a lack of entrepreneurial resource was a major cause of economic stagnation in less developed countries (LDCs). It has become apparent, however, that the development experience of Third World countries in recent decades does not confirm this pessimistic estimate of entrepreneurship constraints. As Leff summarizes,[29] the problem of the supply of entrepreneurship in LDCs seems to have been "solved," because:

——a number of LDCs have demonstrated sustained high rates of real output growth, especially in the manufacturing sectors where entrepreneurship constraints had been expected to be more severe;

——policy makers in the LDCs have displayed diminishing concern about a possible shortage of entrepreneurship in their countries;

——field research has disclosed abundant evidence that the supply of entrepreneurship has turned out to be highly responsive to economic incentives even in cultures and societies about which social scientists had been pessimistic.

These developments indicate the exaggeration of earlier theoretical concerns that the lack of entrepreneurial capacity would be a serious barrier for economic development. It has become clear that economic development in most current LDCs can proceed without these countries having to wait for a psycho-cultural transformation that would increase the supply of entrepreneurs.

More convincing historical evidence is offered by the drastic contrast in performance between economy-pairs that belong to similar ethic/cultural backgrounds but different economic systems. Examples in the post-World War II history are the East-West Germanies, North-South Koreas, Mainland China-Taiwan/Hong Kong, etc. The development experience in those regions supports the proposition that the supply of entrepreneurship is sensitive to differences in economic incentive systems.

The evidence appears to support the "economist's view" of entrepreneurship, but certainly deny neither the impact of non-economic factors on the supply of entrepreneurship nor entrepreneurship as a cause of economic growth and development. What Wilken and other economists' studies have shown is that entrepreneurship "was a cause [of economic growth] in proportion to the favorableness of the economic, social, cultural, and political conditions" that characterized the societies in consideration.[30] The economic conditions appeared to be the most important. Therefore, in most cases, inadequate supply of entrepreneurship should not be a fundamental exogenous obstacle to economic growth. Both the supply of entrepreneurship and the occurrence of economic growth can be effectively influenced by changes in the opportunity conditions, especially the economic incentive system. This conclusion has an important policy implication. It suggests that

> "Without awaiting a change in the entrepreneurial drive exhibited in our society, we can learn how one can stimulate the volume and intensity of entrepreneurial activity, thus making the most of what is permitted by current mores and attitudes."[31]

2.4 The Need to Identify Entrepreneurial Activities

Once the emphasis of the research is directed toward finding appropriate policy actions to operationally stimulate the supply of entrepreneurship, we need to be careful not to take the potential benefits of entrepreneurship for granted. Most social scientists seem to have shared an implicit presumption that productive entrepreneurship is the only form of the phenomenon. This belief has simplified the problem of entrepreneurship to a problem of volume and intensity rather than of quality and direction.

The source of this implicit presumption can be traced back to most of the early theories of entrepreneurship, which have painted a very sanguine and positive picture of the phenomenon. Schumpeter's innovative entrepreneur, Knight's risk-bearing entrepreneur, and Kirzner's opportunity-alert entrepreneur are all heroic figures in economic development, who always enhance social welfare and productive efficiency. As pointed out by M. Marrese, in real life, "entrepreneurship is more complex than this [positive] picture, and contains potentially damaging consequences."[32] For instance, one of the development problems of LDCs is the new economic distortions due to the market power generated by successful entrepreneurship.[33] An acute dilemma for the governments in many LDCs is whether to allow entrepreneurs to expand without restriction or to attempt to correct the economic distortions and the associated social imbalances such as widening disparities in income distribution.[34] The same dilemma is also observed in the process of economic transition toward a market economy in some former centrally-planned economies. The social environment of the emerging private sector has resulted in malpractice of some entrepreneurs, such as myopic business behavior, commercial and financial cheating, the use of bribery in the acquisition of necessary inputs, and so forth.[35] These consequences of entrepreneurial activity need to be better understood.

The presumption that entrepreneurship can never do harm to society prevails the field of research. This presumption inhibits a comprehensive understanding of the role and nature of entrepreneurship. The quality and direction of entrepreneurship, like its volume and intensity, are determined by economic institutions as well as psycho-cultural backgrounds. As noted by J. Hughes, there are four objective determinants of entrepreneurial action: the institutional environment, established rights to property, economic change external to the individual entrepreneur, and technological progress. Success of private gains comes from "the adroit exploitation and manipulation of profit possibilities arising from changes in these variables."[36] There is no guarantee that these objective determinants would always make profit-driven entrepreneurs improve social welfare with their exploitation of existing disequilibria or the creation of new disequilibria. In reality, illegal activities such as drug trafficking and other organized crime, and legal activities such as lobbying for favorable legislation, are all entrepreneurial activities designed to exploit existing disequilibria or create new disequilibria in pursuit of private gains. These activities waste productive resources and result in deadweight losses to society.

The presumption causes theoretical confusion, too. Without distinguishing different types of entrepreneurial activities, most studies in the field have focused on delineating the nature of successful entrepreneurs according to their common personality or behavioral characteristics. These efforts usually distill entrepreneurship into psychological, behavioral, or cultural elements. Throughout history, however, the waxing and waning of productive entrepreneurial activities have not been simply due to cultural or psychological phenomena. Such changes have occurred much more frequently and drastically than the evolution of citizens' psychological attitudes, behavioral patterns, and cultural environment. Accordingly, the elements associated with the common personality or behavioral characteristics of entrepreneurs seem to be neutral or controversially related to the productive aspects of entrepreneurship. This is because these elements are either potentially possessed by almost everyone, or belong only to certain ethnical or cultural groups. Without referring to different uses of entrepreneurial resources, these elements alone are not sufficient to explain why entrepreneurship may improve social welfare, why the intensity of (productive) entrepreneurial activity may vary drastically in the same society, and why welfare impact of entrepreneurship can be very different under different institutional environments. Therefore, the role of entrepreneurial activity remains a mystery.

From there the presumption limits the possibility of drawing policy implications from the literature of entrepreneurship. Since entrepreneurial activity is presumed to automatically play a productive role in socioeconomic development, most scholars in the field treat their work as studies of the availability, rather than the allocation, of the entrepreneurial resources. Besides revealing some psychological, behavioral, or cultural elements of entrepreneurship, such studies provide little guidance to policy makers, because the availability of most of these elements is exogenously determined by factors beyond the influence of policy-making and economic institutions. Therefore, it is very difficult, especially for economists, to relate the research of entrepreneurship to policy issues and draw operational policy conclusions.

To find ways to encourage entrepreneurial activities that benefit society, we have to identify different socioeconomic roles of entrepreneurship. It is also important to explore how institutional determinants interact with entrepreneurial behavior.

2.5 A Taxonomy of Entrepreneurial Activities

In a steady, well-ordered market, equilibrating or innovative entrepreneurship, based on individuals' pursuit of self-interest, acts like the "invisible hand" described by Adam Smith,[37] playing a socially beneficial role. This is the familiar picture of entrepreneurial activity. Buchanan describes this kind of activity as "profit-seeking"(or "rent creation").[38]

Buchanan also points out that similar self-interest seeking behavior under a different set of institutions may not produce socially beneficial consequences. The term "rent-seeking" is designed to "describe behavior in institutional settings where individual efforts to maximize value [of their income] generate social waste rather than social surplus."[39] One of the rent-seeking activities he illustrates is the attempt to capture artificially contrived advantageous positions under officially enforced monopoly. This kind of "competition" among rent seekers for some artificially contrived monopolistic profit may generate not social benefit, but waste. G. Tullock describes this situation as a negative-sum game to society. As he points out, in a "sufficiently badly organized society," individuals' efforts to pursue their own interests are institutionally guided in such a way that they not only waste their own resources, but also impose costs on the rest of society and thus retard development.[40]

In a similar vein, J. Bhagwati proposes "directly unproductive, profit-seeking (DUP) activities" as a general concept that embraces a wide range of economic activities, including rent-seeking activities as a subset.[41] He defines DUP activities as those that yield pecuniary returns (to the seekers) but do not produce / increase goods or services available to society. Four types of DUP activities are characterized by Bhagwati as follows:

1. Both the initial and final situations are distorted (suboptimal). In this case, some kind of (suboptimal) government regulation is in place in the initial situation. Individuals or firms seek benefits from the institution but their actions do not change the nature of the regulation. Examples are: revenue seeking, the legal directly unproductive competition for securing a share in the transfer of tax revenue; tax

evasion, which reduces tax revenue but does not destroy the taxation mechanism.

2. The initial situation is distorted, but the final situation is distortion free (optimal). Here, the initial (suboptimal) regulation is destroyed by individuals' or firms' directly unproductive activity. Examples are: lobbying that successfully removes the regulation, or bribery and black market trade that entirely neutralizes the effects of the regulation.

3. The initial situation is distortion free, but the final situation is distorted. A market distortion is set up by DUP activity here. Examples are: firms' unproductive activity to seek a monopoly position secured by administrative protection; tax evasion from an optimal taxation situation.

4. Both the initial and final situations are distortion free. Examples are: futile lobbying efforts for different purposes that offset each other, ending with no new regulation imposed; law suits; theft and anti-theft activities.

Buchanan and Tullock's rent-seeking theory and Bhagwati's taxonomy of DUP have shed light on a comprehensive understanding of the nature of entrepreneurial activity. Entrepreneurial activities, which originated from particular qualities of human nature, act as equilibrating or innovative (disequilibrating) forces in the market. In many cases, they improve social welfare by improving technology, creating new organization, reforming institutions, filling gaps during disequilibria, exploiting arbitrage opportunities, coordinating, bearing risks, and so forth. In these cases, they can be labeled as "socially beneficial" or "profit-seeking" entrepreneurship. Under certain institutional constraints, however, similar entrepreneurial activities may become socially wasteful rent-seeking activities. Marrese refers to this kind of entrepreneurial activity as "entry-securing" in the sense that it involves the use of resources to secure the right to engage in an activity that generates an "economic rent."[42]

Fung distinguishes two types of economic rent generated by regulatory institution.[43] One is "contrived rent" and the other is "contrived surplus." "Contrived rent" refers to the monopolistic profit that results from restricting market entry and is created to confer benefits on a selected few. "Contrived surplus" refers to the surplus that results from restricting the freedom to set prices and is usually created to facilitate a more even allocation of goods and services in short supply.

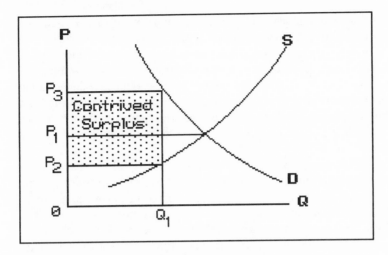

Figure 2.5 Contrived Surplus in a Suppressed Market

The case of contrived rent is similar to that of monopoly profit except that entry is restricted by regulation or other non-market mechanism. Figure 2.5 shows the situation of contrived surplus under a price control. P_1 is the equilibrium price without the price control. P_2 is the price ceiling imposed by regulation. Q_1 is the quantity supplied at P_2. P_3 is the market clearing price under the price control. $(P_3 - P_2)Q_1$ is the contrived surplus. It can be interpreted as consumer surplus of those consumers who are lucky enough to buy the good at the controlled price P_2 or as a turnover tax revenue with a tax rate equal to $(P_3 - P_2)$.

In the case of contrived rent generated by restricted entry, it is usually legal for the monopolistic seller to capture the rent by charging the market-clearing price. Therefore, contrived-rent-seeking activity mainly involves endeavors to create institutional structures to restrict entry, or efforts to enter a restricted market. The activity directed toward creating entry-restriction causes market distortion. This distortion-causing activity is entrepreneurial in the sense that it is disequilibrating and institutionally innovative. This distortion-causing activity functions similarly to Bhagwati's type three DUP ("initially distortion-free but finally distorted situations"). On the other hand, potential competitors' effort to enter the restricted market is a distortion-induced activity in the sense that it occurs under an already-existing distortion. This entry seeking activity is a disequilibrium-gap-filling (equilibrating) entrepreneurial activity but generates social cost as it tries to break the restriction barrier. Since it leads to the destruction of the restriction, it is a "distortion-correcting" activity and works similarly to Bhagwati's type two DUP ("initially distorted but finally distortion-free"). Both distortion-causing and distortion-induced activities can be socially wasteful because they shift the production possibilities frontier inward by wasting productive resources to secure entry.

In the case of contrived surplus, it is usually illegal for the seller to capture the surplus by charging the market-clearing price or evading the turnover tax. So the suppliers' contrived-surplus-seeking efforts focus on disguising such attempts. The activity is distortion-induced and tends to correct the distortion. Therefore it is also a distortion-correcting activity. As suppliers try to charge the market-clearing price, their activity is equilibrating. At the same time it is accompanied with welfare loss since it wastes resources to secure access to the illegal profits.

There is another type of distortion-induced activity aiming to secure access to the contrived surplus. It applies to individuals who try to buy the good at the official price ceiling or to attain the contrived surplus represented by some turnover tax revenue. For example, buyers' queuing efforts to buy goods at the official price are distortion induced. The resources (the queuer's time) spent in this type of rent-seeking activity does not increase the real price facing the suppliers, so the action does not tend to correct the distortion. This type of "distortion-supported" activity is similar to Bhagwati's type one DUP ("initially distorted and finally distorted situations"). The distortion-supported activity is still entrepreneurial in the sense of its disequilibrium-gap-filling function.

A taxonomy of entrepreneurial activities in Figure 2.6 summarizes the above discussion. Generally speaking, entrepreneurial activities may be identified as equilibrating and disequilibrating. Under different institutional settings, these activities may be socially beneficial or wasteful. The socially beneficial activities are profit-seeking while the socially wasteful ones are rent-seeking (or entry-securing). If there is no market distortion, entrepreneurial activities usually benefit society. Disequilibrating profit-seeking activity is called "Schumpeterian," and includes all activities related to efficiency enhancement: technology innovation, organization creation, market opening, and institution reforming. The equilibrating activity is "Kirznerian," and relates to disequilibrium-gap-filling, which includes all forms of coordination, arbitrage, speculation, and hedging behavior.

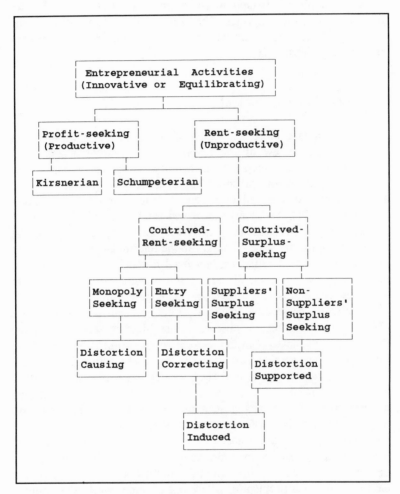

Figure 2.6 A Taxonomy of Entrepreneurial Activities

Rent-seeking (or entry-securing) activities relate to market distortion or market suppression. The two major rent-seeking activities are contrived-rent-seeking and contrived-surplus-seeking. Contrived-rent-seeking involves entry restriction. One type of contrived-rent-seeking is monopoly seeking, which causes the distortion; the other type is entry seeking, which is induced by the distortion and tends to correct the distortion. Contrived-surplus-seeking involves price controls. Suppliers' attempts to charge the market clearing price are distortion-correcting activities. The non-supplier efforts to catch the surplus are distortion-supported activities. Both activities are responses to some initial distortion.

2.6 Concluding Comments

This chapter explores the nature of entrepreneurship on the basis of a literature review of the research field. Entrepreneurship, as economic behavior, refers to the activity to start new businesses, initiate new production processes, or create new organizations. The activity may be innovative or equilibrating in view of market equilibrium. The taxonomy presented above provides a broad perspective on entrepreneurial activities and suggests a functional approach toward the issue. Contrary to the traditional presumption that all entrepreneurial activities are beneficial for society, this perspective has allowed for both positive and negative potentials of entrepreneurial activities regarding social welfare and economic institutions.

Under this perspective, the issue of entrepreneurship identification becomes less puzzling and obscure. As self-interest seeking behavior that creates business opportunities, entrepreneurship is based on the potential human characteristics of alertness to opportunities, imagination of success, and courage to bear risks. Entrepreneurship may act either as a disequilibrating or equilibrating force in the economy. As actions undertaken within the existing structures of institutional environments, entrepreneurial activities do not necessarily guarantee socially beneficial consequences. The significance of entrepreneurship (or the supply of entrepreneurship) should therefore be treated as a problem of the *types* of entrepreneurial activities to be supplied in a socioeconomic environment, or a problem of *allocation* of entrepreneurial resources between socially-beneficial uses and socially-wasteful uses.

The merit of this functional approach to the study of entrepreneurship addresses not only the clarification of the confusion about the two major issues in the literature, but also the possibility to draw policy implications from the literature. If the supply of entrepreneurship is treated only as a problem of availability, rather than allocation of the entrepreneurial resources, a society's vigor of productive entrepreneurship will be at the mercy of some predetermined social factors, such as cultural heritage and ethnic characteristics, which are exogenously to the economic institutions and beyond the control of policy makers. A recent study by Baumol challenges this traditional view of entrepreneurship with abundant historical evidence.[44] According to his argument, the "rules of the game" that specify the relative payoffs to different entrepreneurial activities can significantly affect the vigor of economic growth because they play a key role in determining whether entrepreneurial resources will be allocated in productive or unproductive directions. Therefore, rather than waiting for factors exogenous to economic institutions to slowly increase the available resources of entrepreneurship, one may actively implement institutional changes of the "rules of the game" to improve the allocation of existing entrepreneurial resources. To scrutinize the "rules of the game," the functional approach to the study of entrepreneurship aims to identify different uses of entrepreneurial resources (or different types of entrepreneurial activities) and their corresponding market conditions. The taxonomy of entrepreneurial activities in this chapter may serve as a guideline to identify the institutional factors that encourage productive (socially-beneficial) entrepreneurship and therefore to generate constructive policy suggestions.

Figure 2.7 illustrates the novelty of the functional approach. The upper part of the graph shows the traditional perspective on the role of entrepreneurial activities. Without distinguishing different types of entrepreneurial activities, the intensity of [productive] entrepreneurship appears to be exogenously determined outside the economic institutions. There seems little policy-makers can do to change the availability of a society's entrepreneurial resources. The lower part of the graph shows the functional approach to the study of entrepreneurship. The social welfare effects of entrepreneurship are considered dependent on whether society's entrepreneurial resources are allocated to productive uses or unproductive uses. The mechanism of entrepreneurial resource allocation, however, is institutionally defined. Therefore, the welfare effects of entrepreneurial activities are highly sensitive to institutional arrangements, or the "rules of the game," which are subject to policy changes. Meanwhile, this functional approach does not deny that non-economic, social-cultural factors are important in determining the availability of a society's entrepreneurial resources.

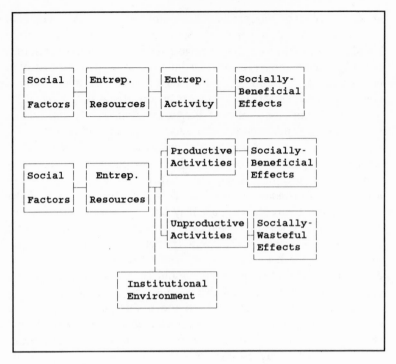

Figure 2.7   Two Perspectives on Entrepreneurial Activities

NOTES

1. Hebert, R. F. and A. N. Link, *The Entrepreneurship: Mainstream Views and Radical Critiques*. New York: Praeger Publishers, CBS Educational and Professional Publishing, 1982, pp. 107-110.

2. Gartner, W. B. op. cit.

3. See Kilby, P. op. cit., R. Hebert and A. Link, op. cit., and Joshua Ronen, "Introduction," *Entrepreneurship*, J. Ronen ed. Lexington, MA: Lexington Books, pp. 1-12, for comments on entrepreneurial personality.

4. Gartner, W. B. op. cit.

5. Wilken, P. H. op. cit.

6. Hebert and Link, op. cit.

7. Cantillon, R., *Essai sur la nature dela commerce en général*. H. Higgs ed., London: Macmillan, 1931 (1755); Knight, F. W., *Risk, Uncertainty and Profit*, New York: Harper and Row, 1965(1921); Mises, L. von, *Human Action: A Treatise of Economics*, New Haven, Conn.: Yale University Press, 1949.

8. Schmöller, G., *The Mercantile System*, New York: Smith, 1891; Weber, Max, *The Protestant Ethic and the Spirit of Capitalism*, translated by T. Parsons, New York: Scribner's, 1930; Schumpeter, J.A., *Capitalism, Socialism and Democracy*, New York: Harper and Row, 1942.

9. Bentham, Jeremy, *Jeremy Bentham's Economic Writings*, John Bowring ed., New York: Russell & Russell, 1952; Thünen, J.M. von. *Isolated State*, Peter Hall ed., Oxford: Pergaman, 1966; Cole, A. H., "An Approach to the Study of Entrepreneurship," *Journal of Economic History*, supp. 6, 1946, pp. 1-15.

10. Clark, John B., "Insurance and Business Profits," *Quarterly Journal of Economics*, Vol. 7, 1892, pp. 45-54; Clark, John B., *Essentials of*

Economic Theory, New York: Macmillan, 1907; Kirzner, I. M., *Perception, Opportunity, and Profit*, Chicago: The University of Chicago Press, 1979; Schultz, Theodore W., "The Value of the Ability to Deal With Disequilibria," *Journal of Economic Literature*, Vol.13, 1975, pp. 827-46.

11. Hebert and Link, op. cit., pp. 111-114.

12. Leibenstein, Harvey, "Entrepreneurship and Development," *American Economic Review*, Vol.52, no.2, 1968, pp. 72-83.

13. Hayek, F. A., "Economics and Knowledge," *Economica* (N.S.), Vol.4, 1937, pp. 33-54; *Individualism and Economic Order*, London: Routledge and Kegan Paul, 1959; *The Constitution of Liberty*, Chicago: University of Chicago Press, 1960.

14. Kirzner, op. cit.

15. Casson, Mark, *The Entrepreneur: An Economic Theory*, Totowa, New Jersey: Barnes & Noble Books, 1982.

16. Schumpeter, op. cit.

17. Hughes, op. cit., p. 214.

18. Daniel W. Bromley explains how institutional change can re-shape a society's production possibilities and technical choice. See Bromley, D., "Institutional Change and Economic Efficiency," *Journal of Economic Issues*, Vol.23, no.3, Sept. 1989, pp. 735-759.

19. Kilby, op. cit. pp. 3-5.

20. Fairbairn, op. cit. p. 21.

21. Kilby, op. cit.

22. Kirzner, op. cit.

23. Hayek, 1959, 1960, op. cit.

24. Kirzner, op. cit.

25. An economic literature about entrepreneurial activities has emerged. For instance, see Kihlstrom and Laffont's model of entrepreneurship [Kihlstrom, R. E. and J. Laffont, "A General Equilibrium Entrepreneurial Theory of Firm Formation Based on Risk Aversion," *Journal of Political Economy*, Vol.87, no.4, 1979, pp. 719-748]; Casson's framework of an economic theory about entrepreneurial coordination (Casson, op. cit.); D. Diamond's model about risk-neutral entrepreneurs' role in financial intermediation [Diamond, D., "Financial Intermediation and Delegated Monitoring," *Review of Economic Studies*, Vol.51, July 1984, pp. 393-414]; Baumol's model of supply of entrepreneurship [Baumol, W., "Toward Operational Models of Entrepreneurship," in *Entrepreneurship*, J. Ronen ed. Lexington, MA: Lexington Books, 1983, pp. 28-48)]; Grossman and Hart's comparative study between classical entrepreneur-controlled firm and alternative forms of organization [Grossman, S. and O. Hart, "The Cost And Benefits of Ownership: A Theory of Vertical And Lateral Integration," *Journal of Political Economy*, Vol.94, 1986, pp. 691-719]. More examples can be found in Libecap, G. ed. *Advances in the Study of Entrepreneurship, Innovation, and Economic Growth*, Vol. 1-2. Greenwood, CT: JAI Press, 1987-88.

26. Wilken, op. cit.

27. Fairbairn, op. cit., pp. 20-21.

28. Wilken, op. cit.

29. Leff, N. H., "Entrepreneurship and Economic Development: the Problem Revisited," *Journal of Economic Literature*, Vol. 17, 1979, pp. 46-64.

30. Wilken, op. cit., p. 280.

31. Baumol, William J. ,"Entrepreneurship in Economic Theory," *American Economic Review*, Vol. 58, no. 2, 1968, pp. 64-71 [p. 71].

32. Marrese, M. op. cit.

33. Mason, Edward S., "Monopolistic Competition and the Growth Process in Less Developed Countries: Chamberlin and the Schumpeterian Dimension," in *Monopolistic Competition Theory: Studies in Impact*, R.E. Kuenne ed. New York: Wiley, 1967, pp. 77-104.

34. Leff, op. cit., p. 55.

35. Kornai, János, "The Affinity Between Ownership Forms and Coordination Mechanisms: The Common Experience of Reform in Socialist Countries," *Journal of Economic Perspectives*, Vol. 4, no. 3, 1990, pp. 131-147.

36. Hughes, op. cit., p. 215.

37. Smith, Adam, *The Wealth of Nations,* New York: Random House, Modern Library Edition, 1937.

38. Buchanan, J. M., "Rent Seeking and Profit Seeking," in *Toward a Theory of the Rent-Seeking Society*, J. M. Buchanan, R. D. Tollison, G. Tullock, ed. U.S.A.: Texas A & M University Press, 1980, pp. 3-15.

39. Buchanan, op. cit., p. 4.

40. Tullock, G., "Rent Seeking as a Negative-Sum Game," in *Toward a Theory of the Rent-Seeking Society*, J.M. Buchanan, R.D. Tollison, G. Tullock. ed., U.S.A.: Texas A & M University Press, 1980, pp. 16-36.

41. Bhagwati, J. N. op. cit.

42. Marrese, M. op. cit.

43. Fung, K. K., "Surplus Seeking and Rent Seeking Through Back-Door Deals in Mainland China," *American Journal of Economics and Sociology*, Vol. 46, no. 3, 1987, pp. 299-317.

44. Baumol, W., 1990, op. cit.

CHAPTER 3

OPPORTUNITIES
IN SUPPRESSED MARKETS

3.1 Introduction

In the preceding chapter, we note that the role of entrepreneurship is sensitive to institutional settings. As pointed out by Baumol, entrepreneurship can be productive, unproductive, or even destructive, depending on the "rules of the game," or institutional settings.[1] We therefore propose a functional approach to the study of entrepreneurship in the context of economic institutions. This chapter analyzes how the role of entrepreneurial activity varies in suppressed markets.

Market suppression may occur when administrative instruments are used to impose a resource allocation other than the laissez-faire market outcome. Government intervention of free market equilibrium is justifiable given that such intervention is based on true market failures. It is very important, however, to be aware that the use of government's visible hand is itself a costly process. The intervention is cost-effective only when the *net* improvement of society's welfare is positive. In other words, society's finally-improved welfare should exceed all the costs, direct or indirect, arising from the use of administrative instruments. Otherwise, the intervention would be a government failure.

One indirect cost of government intervention is the welfare loss due to unproductive entrepreneurial activities, which are induced by the contrived benefits in a suppressed market. Several writers have noticed that when markets are suppressed or distorted by government intervention entrepreneurial activity may generate social waste. For example, Alm points out that a tax on a productive factor in only some of its uses will generate a welfare cost. Inefficiency arises as the taxation encourages over-allocation of resources to untaxed activities.[2]

The Peruvian economist Hernando de Soto argues that regulations which force entrepreneurs underground have generated significant social waste in Third World countries.[3] He recommends the legalization of underground or informal economies as a recipe for growth in underdeveloped economies. In the context of reformed centrally-planned economies, Marrese discusses the possibility of an entrepreneurial activity that wastes resources   the "entry-securing" activity. This rent-seeking activity involves the use of resources to secure the right to engage in an activity that generates an "economic rent" due to a market distortion.[4]

Market suppression may take the form of regulatory control in a market economy. The most revealing case of market suppression, however, exists in the centrally-planned economy. Section 3.2 discusses how suppression of free market operation may generate market disequilibria and consequently create rents or contrived surplus. In particular, we will identify two types of suppressed markets and the resulting deadweight losses to social welfare in a hypothetical planned economy. Section 3.3 deals with the opportunities for innovative entrepreneurship in suppressed markets. Section 3.4 describes the rent-seeking cost associated with equilibrating entrepreneurship in a suppressed market. The last section summarizes the findings of the chapter.

3.2 Disequilibria in Suppressed Markets

Despite the specific forms of the administrative intervention, market suppression essentially involves distorted prices or cost structures that deviate from market-clearing prices. The source of market suppression can be illustrated by a simplified model of Kantorovich planning.[5] Kantorovich was an economist who advocated that planners use shadow prices to guide enterprises to attain a planned equilibrium. There are several assumptions of the model:

(1) There are only two goods in an economy: B ("Butter") and G ("Gun").

(2) "Labor," a perfectly mobile factor input with a fixed total amount, is used in both sectors of butter industry and gun industry.

(3) In both sectors, production is subject to diminishing returns so that the social production-possibilities frontier is well defined.

(4) The demand of the populace for the two goods possesses the normal properties of a utility function of the populace.

(5) The producers of both goods make their decisions on their own according to the price signals.

Given these assumptions, it can be shown that the free market equilibrium would occur when a set of prices "clear" both markets, i.e., quantity demanded and quantity supplied would be equal at both markets. At market equilibrium, the marginal rate of substitution [6] and the marginal rate of transformation[7] would be equal to each other.

Now suppose that there is a central planner who aims to achieve a type of allocation it believes to be superior to the market equilibrium. Based on his preferences, the planner wants to produce more "guns" than that would be produced in a market equilibrium. Given the resource constraint, the economy has to produce less "butter" than that would have been produced at market equilibrium. Since the producers make their decisions on their own, the central planners cannot simply order them to produce his preferred output mix. If, however, the central planner can somehow raise the price faced by the gun producers relative to that faced by the butter producers, he can then use the price incentive to induce the producers to achieve what he wants. By simple economic reasoning, to induce gun producers to produce more guns than the level at a market equilibrium, the gun price facing the gun producers must rise above the free market price level. Similarly, to induce less butter production, the planned price of butter must be lower than the free market level. These centrally-planned producer prices are "shadow prices" advocated by Kantorovich.

The consumer preferences and the consequent demand for the two goods, however, did not change at all. Furthermore, in the "gun" market, with a higher-than-equilibrium supply of "gun," the market clearing price should be even lower than the market equilibrium price (see Figure 3.1). By similar reason, in the "butter" market, the market clearing price with a lower-than-equilibrium supply of "butter" should be higher than the market equilibrium price of "butter." There exists a gap between the centrally-planned producer price and the market clearing price in both markets.

How does the central planner impose the shadow prices? It may set the planned shadow prices as the only legal prices in the two markets. It may otherwise set them as the wholesale prices facing producers and make the legal retail prices closed to the market clearing prices. The government then imposes a turnover tax between wholesale and retail prices. In a partial equilibrium context, these planning schemes result in two types of price distortion: one is a supported price (the price floor) in the "gun" market (Figure 3.1), the other is a suppressed price (the price ceiling) in the "butter" market (Figure 3.2).

In both markets, the price distortion generates some static deadweight loss to the economy. In the "gun" market, a planned price floor p^f is arranged for producers. Let the demand function be $D(p)$ and the supply function be $S(p)$. As $S(p^f) > D(p^f)$, the government must either, while enforcing p^f as the official price in the market, subsidize consumers to induce them to buy up the excess supply at p^f; or, while letting the market-clearing price be the retail price, subsidize producers to supply the quantity $S(p^f)$. Define the market equilibrium price p^* such that $D(p^*) - S(p^*) = 0$, and p^{mf} such that $D(p^{mf}) - S(p^f) = 0$. Producer surplus increases by the area c-d-e-f. The consumer surplus increases by the area a-b-c-d. The government subsidy is, however, $(p^f - p^{mf})S(p^f)$, the area a-b-e-f, and exceeds the total increase in consumer and producer surplus. The deadweight loss to society is then the shaded area (b-c-f) in Figure 3.1.

In the "butter" market, where an official price ceiling p^l is imposed, there is a shortage $D(p^l) - S(p^l)$. Define p^{ml} as the market clearing price such that $D(p^{ml}) - S(p^l) = 0$. The area a-b-e-f, $(p^{ml} - p^l)S(p^l)$, represents the contrived surplus. This surplus may be obtained by the consumers who manage to buy the goods at the price p^l, or by the producers who successfully sell their goods at the market clearing price.[8] The direct deadweight loss to society is then the net loss of consumer and producer surplus, which is the shaded area b-f-g in Figure 3.2.

The results of the Kantorovich model are relevant not only to the hypothetical central-planning scenario proposed by Kantorovich. In a real-world centrally-planned command economy like the former Soviet Union, producers were mainly state-owned enterprises that received production commands from the central planning authorities. Nevertheless, the central planners still had to worry about providing proper incentives to these enterprises. Enterprises that produced priority goods (such as those in heavy industries) were usually subsidized by the government. While in non-priority industries goods and services were generally under-priced and shortage prevails. Similar deviations of planned prices from market equilibrium level also exist in many regulated markets in capitalist countries. These distorted prices usually involve contrived benefits and deadweight losses to society.

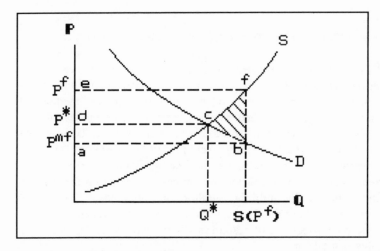

Figure 3.1 The "Gun" Market
The price floor p^f is the centrally-planned producer price. The price p^* is the equilibrium price. The priice p^{mf} is the market clearing price when the quantity supplied is $S(p^f)$.

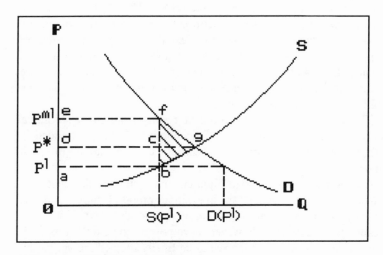

Figure 3.2 The "Butter" Market
The price ceiling p^l is the centrally-planned producer price. The price p^* is the equilibrium price. The priice p^{ml} is the market clearing price when the quantity supplied is $S(p^l)$.

3.3 Innovative Entrepreneurship: Chance and Impact

The role of entrepreneurial activity in the marketplace can be identified as innovative or equilibrating. Innovative entrepreneurs, as described by Schumpeter,[9] introduce novel products and methods of production, open untouched markets, exploit new sources of raw material, and find creative ways to organize an industry. Their actions cause changes to the production function, start the process of "creative-destruction," and produce disequilibrating changes. Equilibrating entrepreneurship, as considered by Kirzner,[10] is based on the reaction of individuals to disequilibria. Equilibrating entrepreneurs are alert to disequilibria and are the first to respond to excess demand by altering the accepted allocation of resources. Both types of entrepreneurship involve risk taking.

Under central planning, the chances for innovative entrepreneurship are usually slim. There are two sources of this problem. One stems from miscalculation on the part of the central planners. In the former Soviet Union, for instance, the political elite believed that centralization of highly specialized R & D activities would eliminate duplication of effort and take advantage of economic scale.[11] The centralized R & D system, however, lacked the competition that would vitalize innovation in market economies. The system also did not generate multiple independent sources of funding for innovation as does a market economy. Innovators under the system were also deprived of the chance of enjoying windfall gains once the innovation materialized as they would have in a market economy.

The other source of the problem results from the institutional features of the centrally-planned economies. Levine provided a synthesis of the institutional obstacles to innovation in such economies.[12]

(a) A strict, authoritarian hierarchy characterizes the centrally-planned economies. When an innovative proposal moves up the hierarchy, each approval merely moves it to the next level. The bureaucrats at each level, however, have powers to veto the proposal. Therefore, the chances of proposal to be finally adopted are very slim.

(b) These economies tend to create narrowly specialized ministries designed to take advantage of economies of scale. The system encourages these ministries to fulfill their own plan targets but provides little incentive for them to mind the externalities outside one's ministry.

It is usually very difficult to cross ministrial boundaries to develop new production process. The separation between R & D and production within each ministry also acts as a barrier to the transfer of new technology from laboratory to production.

(c) Under central planning, bureaucrats are penalized more for failure than they are rewarded for success. They therefore fear the many uncertainties that surround innovation and appreciate routine, non-stressful fulfillment of plan targets. This results in a high degree of risk aversion toward innovation.

(d) The managerial reward mechanism in these economies has a "ratchet effect": The central authorities adjust plan targets according the previous performance of the enterprise. The success today means a higher target tomorrow. The maintenance of managerial status requires the rather regular meeting of targets. Thus the managers resist innovation and try to keep targets low. The short-run disruption of current production caused by introduction of an innovation is also a threat to managers' reward and status.

(e) The more accurate the central planning is, the tighter the mandatory targets and planned quota of raw material supply. To ensure an easy job to meet the plan targets, the managers tend to demand excess inputs for production. The absence of slack on both the demand side and the supply side inhibits the introduction of new technology.

(f) Enterprises do not have control over the price of new products. They are isolated from the real market demand because the state control of price setting. There is simply no demand pressure to innovate.

(g) Enterprises in these economies do not face the fear of being driven out of business by competition.

Not only is the chance for innovative entrepreneurship much smaller in a suppressed market but also has the role of this type of entrepreneurship changed. The main role of innovative entrepreneurs is the introduction of a new production function characterized by more efficient use of resources and lower production costs. As discussed in Section 2.2, this can be represented by an outward shift of the market supply curve. It is no doubt that an outward shift of supply curve in a free market benefit society. In a suppressed market, however, the role of innovative entrepreneurship is ambiguous, depending on the type of market distortion. In Figure 3.3, in a market with a price floor (p^f), the market clearing price is p^{mf}. An innovation reduces the marginal production cost such that the supply curve shifts outward by θ. The new supply is $\hat{S}(p) = S(p) + \theta$. The shift out of the supply curve will increase the shaded (triangle) area that represents the deadweight loss to society.

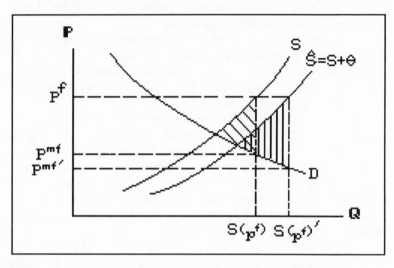

Figure 3.3 Innovative Activity in a Market with a Price Floor

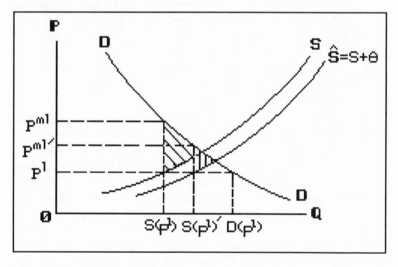

Figure 3.4 Innovative Activity in a Market with a Price Ceiling

In contrast, an innovative activity plays a more beneficial role in a market with a price ceiling. Figure 3.4 shows that the innovative activity reduces the static deadweight loss to society. As the supply curve shifts out, the shaded (triangle) area shrinks.

The existence of rent-seeking opportunities also affect the chance of innovative activity. A recent study by Murphy, Shleifer, and Vishny suggests that political rent-seeking tends to attack the innovative activity more severely than it does to routine production.[13] These authors describe private rent-seeking as forms of transfer between private parties, including theft, piracy, litigation, etc. The public rent-seeking, is either redistribution from the private sector to the state, or alternatively from the private sector to the government bureaucrats who affect the fortunes of private entrepreneurs. Since private rent-seekers go after existing stocks of wealth, such as land, output, capital, and so on, they attack the established producers rather than the innovators. On the other hand, innovators, usually as new producers, need government-supplied goods, such as permits, licenses, etc., much more so than the established producers. Such demand for government-supplied goods is high and inelastic when new businesses start. New producers hence become primary targets of corruption. They are also more vulnerable to public rent-seeking than the established producers because they have no established lobbies, are more credit-constrained, and involve longer term of investment and higher risks.

3.4 Equilibrating Entrepreneurship and Rent Dissipation

In a distortion-free market, when market conditions change, equilibrating entrepreneurs react to adjust the quantity supplied and move the market to a new equilibrium. When the market is suppressed by a controlled price, such a gap-filling role is eliminated.

As shown in Figure 3.5 (a) and (b), when market demand changes, as long as the change does not generate a market equilibrium price higher than the price floor in case (a) or lower than the price ceiling in case (b), the reaction of supply adjustment is totally suppressed.

Even worse, when market suppression generates some contrived surplus or rent, entrepreneurial activity may become socially wasteful as entrepreneurs employ extra resources to secure access to the surplus. In an extreme case of rent-seeking [as suggested by Posner] the total expense by individuals or firms to obtain the rent is equal to the amount of the monopolistic rent.[14] The following case illustrates how, in a suppressed market with a price ceiling, the contrived surplus may be fully dissipated as a pure waste.

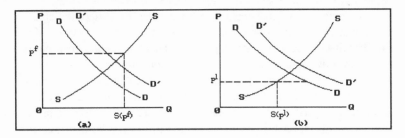

Figure 3.5 Suppressed Market Signals

Case 1. In a market suppressed by a price ceiling p^l, firms are effectively banned from supplying their products on the black market at the market clearing price but arbitrage between consumers is possible. A shortage exists as the difference between $D(p^l)$ and $S(p^l)$. The purchase of each unit of the good at official price generates a contrived surplus $p^{ml} - p^l$ [see Figure 3.3]. The equilibrating entrepreneurs will spend resources to obtain the contrived surplus by purchasing the good at official price and reselling it at market clearing price.

Suppose that the good is sold at the official price on a basis of "one unit per customer" and "first come first served." The queuing problem is a "one line-one server" problem and the arrival of customers and supply of the good occur in accordance with a Poisson process.[15] The only resource an entrepreneur can spend on queuing to buy the good at the official price is his time available for making money. It is then easy to show that the social search cost of the contrived surplus under a price ceiling is equal to the amount of the surplus, given that the good in shortage is sold on a basis of "one unit per customer" and "first come first served." (A more rigorous proof is enclosed in the appendix to this chapter.) Here, the contrived surplus is fully dissipated as a pure waste because the way resource (time) spent on seeking the surplus (queuing) is unproductive from society's point of view.

As Fisher and Tirole point out, the plausibility of Posner's extreme case of fully wasteful rent dissipation depends on a number of restrictive institutional assumptions.[16] The social loss due to rent-seeking activity in the real world varies considerably with the institutional arrangement of rent dissipation.

The next case depicts a more realistic situation where the surplus seeking cost is smaller than the contrived surplus being sought under a price ceiling. The equilibrating activity is still associated with rent-seeking cost but the deadweight loss to society is smaller than that in Case 1.

Case 2. In a market suppressed by a price ceiling, firms are not effectively banned from selling their products at market clearing price in the black market. However, because of the illegality of black market transaction, firms selling in the black market are subject to extra costs. This cost may include the entrepreneurs' precautionary efforts to get around official policing of the black market. Since entrepreneurial firms' activity to supply in the black market is only partially wasteful, the contrived surplus is not fully dissipated as in Case 1. Meanwhile the increased supply, thanks to the black market transaction, has reduced the static deadweight loss shown in Figure 3.2. The deadweight loss, however, still exists. It includes two parts now: One is the deadweight loss due to the lower-than-free-market-equilibrium level caused by the price control. The other is the deadweight loss due to firms' wasteful expense on rent-seeking, the extra costs of supplying in an illegal manner. A more technical exposure of the case can be found in the appendix to this chapter.

If the rent-seeking cost is not fully wasteful but includes some dissipated rent as a transfer payment to other agents, then some part of the loss due to rent-seeking may be "saved" for the transfer payment receivers. The following case illustrates such a possible situation.[17]

Case 3. Suppose in the suppressed market, the economic policing of black market exchange is undertaken by a hierarchic bureaucratic structure. The policing hierarchy is composed of $n+1$ tiers, each of which is under the charge of a single official. Except the top official ($n+1$th), who is really enthusiastic about suppressing the black market, every official is vulnerable to corruption and is supervised by the official at the next higher tier. To make sure that the policing system works, the top official randomly checks along the hierarchy.

Suppose at equilibrium, for every dollar of a black market firm's rent-seeking cost $\phi C_i(q_i)$ [defined in the appendix], a proportion ρ ($0 < \rho < 1$) is spent on real resources to disguise the illegal sale from detection by the random checks from the top official; the remaining ($1 - \rho$) is a bribe paid to the official in charge of the direct policing of the black market transaction (assuming the equilibrium bribe is enough to corrupt the official). For the ith corrupt official, a proportion of bribery income, γ $(0<\gamma<1)$, must be forgone as precautionary spending to protect himself. Of the corrupt official's precautionary spending, the proportion ρ is spent on real resources to escape the random checks from the top official, and $(1-\rho)$ is used as a bribe to the next higher tier official. If the equilibrium values of γ and ρ are the same for all corrupt officials, a chain of bribery spending extends as follows:

$$
1 \!-\!\! \begin{cases} \rho \\ 1-\rho \!-\!\! \begin{cases} (1-\gamma)(1-\rho) \\ \gamma\rho(1-\rho) \\ \gamma(1-\rho) \!-\!\! \begin{cases} \gamma(1-\gamma)(1-\rho)^2 \\ \gamma(1-\rho)^2 \!-\!\! \begin{cases} \gamma^2\rho(1-\rho)^2 \\ \gamma^2(1-\rho)^2 \!-\!\! \begin{cases} \cdots \\ \gamma^2(1-\rho)^3 \end{cases} \end{cases} \end{cases} \end{cases}
$$

$$\cdots$$

The total bribe ratio (B) of every dollar of a firm's precaution cost is

$$
B = (1-\gamma)(1-\rho) + \gamma(1-\gamma)(1-\rho)^2 + \gamma^2(1-\gamma)(1-\rho)^3 + \ldots
$$

$$
= (1-\gamma)(1-\rho)\sum_{i=0}^{n}(1-\rho)^i\gamma^i
$$

$$
= \frac{(1-\gamma)(1-\rho)}{1-(1-\rho)\gamma}
$$

The total real resource spending ratio (Ω) is

$$
\Omega = \rho + \rho(1-\rho)\gamma + \rho(1-\rho)^2\gamma^2 + \ldots
$$

$$
= \rho\sum_{i=0}^{n}(1-\rho)^i\gamma^i
$$

$$
= \frac{\rho}{1-\gamma(1-\rho)}
$$

It is easy to see that $B = 1 - \Omega$.

Therefore, of firm i's rent-seeking cost, only $\Omega\phi C_i(q_i)$ is the real resource cost, while $(1-\Omega)\phi C_i(q_i)$ is a transfer payment (bribe) to the corrupt officials. For the economy as a whole, the real resource cost is $\Omega\phi$ $[C(Q^b+Q^l) - C(Q^l)]$. If one does not consider the external cost of political corruption (for example, the social tension of income redistribution), the increase of the equilibrium bribery ratio B tends to reduce the real resource cost of rent-seeking to society.

It is also plausible that the increase in B may reduce the firms' total rent-seeking cost. As firms spend more money on bribing officials, they tend to get better protection from the latter. If this means that ϕ as well as Ω is reduced, the black market suppliers will then enjoy a lower rent-seeking cost. A less steep supply curve in the black market implies an equilibrium closer to the free market equilibrium, and thus results in a smaller direct deadweight loss to society (area "a" in Figure 3.6). In consequence, the existence of bureaucratic corruption may "lubricate" the operation of equilibrating forces in a suppressed market and provide a "second best" solution to resource allocation in a suppressed market.[18]

3.5 Concluding Comments

This chapter has provided an examination of the opportunity and role of entrepreneurial activity in suppressed markets where disequilibria exist. We have identified two types of disequilibrium: the one in the market suppressed by a price floor and the one in the market suppressed by a price ceiling. There are some obvious limits to this preliminary analysis. First, the market distortion is defined in an abstract sense. There is no distinction between price regulation as a remedy to market failure or as a result of some "government failure." Second, the occurrence of entrepreneurial innovation is presumed. The impact of price distortion on innovative behavior are not explored in depth. Third, the government's cost of imposing price controls and the economic policing of them is not explicitly presented in the calculation of deadweight loss. Finally, the institutional assumptions in the model are somewhat arbitrary.

Despite these reservations, the waste associated with entrepreneurship here represents an important part of the social cost of government regulation and intervention. The key problem identified in this study has its roots in price distortion, which is a reality in regulated market economies as well as in centrally planned economies. No matter what forms of government intervention are in place, the real prices faced by firms and consumers are distorted. The theoretical results obtained above can therefore be supported by a variety of real world evidence. The negative welfare effects of innovative entrepreneurship, for instance, can be observed in the situation where the government budget is heavily burdened by the commitment to subsidize the growth of certain industries. This is especially true when the continuation of such subsidy is no longer considered necessary but its removal is strongly opposed by the related interest groups.

For equilibrating entrepreneurship, the three hypothetical cases of rent-seeking waste discussed above can find empirical examples in traditional and reformed centrally-planned economies such as the former Soviet Union, China, and Hungary. The fully wasteful rent dissipation scenario is consistent with the fact that a major source of the low efficiency of centrally-planned economies can be attributed to the huge waste of labor-hours and other human resources in queuing and searching for consumer goods in shortage. The analysis of this scenario also provides rationale for the rationing of goods and services in these economies. In the scenario of partially wasteful rent dissipation, the experience of the private sector in these economies merits a footnote. The growth of the private sector generally improves social welfare but usually at the cost of wasting real resources to break institutional barriers. The development of private entrepreneurship and the process of economic reform have been characterized not only by legal actions but also, and maybe more frequently, by illegal actions to get around institutional constraints. These actions include black market exchange, bribery and embezzlement, bureaucratic corruption, tax evasion, and other forms of violation of law and regulation. These illegal activities are usually associated with internal costs to firms or external costs to society.

The theoretical results imply that a proper solution to the problem of wasteful rent dissipation in a suppressed market should be the removal of the source of the market distortion rather than increasing the wasteful cost by the imposition of further restrictions on productive entrepreneurial activities. More generally, any policy design of government regulation should take into account the potential welfare effects of the role of entrepreneurial activities. Additional research is clearly needed to study the issue in better specified institutional frameworks and to derive more explicit results for public policy making.

Most (former) centrally-planned economies such as China and Russia are undergoing a transition toward a market economy. Many newly-emerged entrepreneurial activities possess rent-seeking characteristics related to the institutional legacies of the old system. The rent-seeking activities in these economies are far more complicated than the simple cases in this chapter have suggested. To understand these activities, it may be helpful to identify two types of rent-seeking activities in centrally-planned economies.

The first is "horizontal rent seeking," which refers to horizontal transaction of goods or services in shortage among firms or individuals. The cases discussed in this chapter belong to this category. The activity often involves market distortions and disequilibria. It usually takes the forms of illegal or semi-legal actions. The role of this type of entrepreneurial activity is equilibrating and tends to improve resource allocation with some deadweight loss to society. It would not be seen as rent-seeking should the trade be free. Because the activity usually violates the existing laws, it carries rent-seeking costs in forms of individuals' expense on avoiding official policing and crackdowns.

The second type is "vertical rent seeking." In a centrally planned economy, opportunities exist for enterprise managers to use their talents to influence the effective reward rate of their enterprises through negotiation with their supervisory authorities for favorable economic treatments, such as easier-to-reach plan targets, centrally-assigned financial or material resources, and so forth. In a transitional economy, there are still spacious rooms for state-owned enterprises to seek benefits from the government. This type of activity attempts contrived benefits or privileges *vertically* along the hierarchy of the planning apparatus. The consequence is the non-market resource allocation that generates market distortions. It is therefore a "distortion-causing" activity according to the taxonomy presented in Chapter 2. Vertical rent-seeking is unproductive but generally legal in most economies. The activity may occur in a market economy in the form of political lobbying.

APPENDIX

A. Proof of the results of Case 1

The following variables are defined: ----μ (the service rate): the average number of goods supplied on the market in a unit of time [or the average number of buyers who can purchase the good in shortage in a unit of time]. Obviously, μ is a function of the shortage $D(p^l)$-$S(p^l)$ or the level of the price ceiling, $\mu = G(p^l)$, $G' < 0$. The shortage implies that the mean shopping time $1/\mu > 0$. At a free market equilibrium, the good is immediately available, so $1/\mu \approx 0$.
----λ (the arrival rate): the average number of people going to the market in a unit of time. [The queue is not endless, $\therefore \lambda/\mu < 1$.]
----w: the wage rate of a unit of working time, which reflects the marginal productivity of labor in the economy.

By a well-known relationship in queuing theory,[19] the expected number of people in the queue, N_q, is

$$N_q = \frac{\lambda^2}{\mu(\mu-\lambda)}$$

and the average waiting time for each person who wishes to buy a unit of the good is $L_{qi} = N_q/\lambda$. Therefore, the average time a buyer spends on shopping for a unit of the good is the average waiting time plus the mean shopping time

$$L_i = \frac{\lambda}{\mu(\mu-\lambda)} + \frac{1}{\mu} = \frac{1}{\mu-\lambda}$$

A person's expected gain from each unit of time spent on shopping is $(p^{ml} - p^l)/L_i = (p^{ml} - p^l)(\mu - \lambda)$.

By the definition of w, an "average" person's decision to spend an extra unit of time on shopping or working depends on whether he/she expects that $(p^{ml} - p^l)(\mu - \lambda) > w$ or not. If $(p^{ml} - p^l)(\mu - \lambda) > w$, more people will choose to join the queue, so λ grows; if $(p^{ml} - p^l)(\mu - \lambda) \leq$

w, more people will choose to leave the queue for work, so λ declines. Dynamically, λ is determined as

$$\dot{\lambda} \begin{cases} > 0 & \text{if } (p^{ml} - p^l)(\mu - \lambda) > w; \\ \leq 0 & \text{otherwise}. \end{cases}$$

In equilibrium, the average number of buyers shopping for the good in a unit of time will reach a level such that $(p^{ml} - p^l)(\mu - \lambda) = w$, or $(p^{ml} - p^l) = wL_i$. In other words, the economy spends approximately L_i units of time on shopping for one unit of the good in shortage. The total labor hours the economy spends on shopping is then $L^s \equiv L_i S(p^l)$. The total social cost of shopping is $wL^s = S(p^l)(p^{ml} - p^l)$, which is the amount of the surplus.

B. A technical exposure of Case 2

Define Q^l as the total quantity of the good supplied at the official price, $Q^l = S(p^l)$. Black market demand is the residual demand left by the official market, where non-entrepreneurial firms obey the price ceiling:[20]

$$D_b(p) = \begin{cases} D(p) - Q^l, & \text{if } D(p) > Q^l; \\ 0, & \text{otherwise}. \end{cases}$$

Obviously, the price in the black market is bounded by p^l. The entrepreneurial firms react to the shortage by engaging in black market production. Denote q_i as the ith black market firm's quantity of production. The inverse demand function on the black market satisfies

$$Q^b = \sum_{i=1}^{n} q_i \begin{cases} > 0, & \text{if } P(\sum_{i=1}^{n} q_i + Q^l) > p^l; \\ = 0, & \text{otherwise}. \end{cases}$$

Let the production cost function be $C_i(q_i)$ for firm i. As sales on the black market are illegal, the firms bear some extra rent-seeking cost proportional to their production cost $\phi \, C_i(q_i)$, where $\phi \geq 0$. This cost can be interpreted as the firms' precautionary efforts to get around official policing of the black market. Firm i's profit function is

$$\pi^i = P(\sum_{i=1}^{n} q_i + Q^l) q_i - (1+\phi) C_i(q_i)$$

Denote q_{-i} as the quantity supplied by firms other than i. The Cournot equilibrium of firms on the black market yields:

$$\frac{\partial \pi^i}{\partial q_i} = P(q_i + q_{-i} + Q^l) - (1+\phi) C_i'(q_i) + q_i P'(q_i + q$$

We can rewrite this equation as

$$\frac{P - C_i'}{P} = \frac{r_i}{\epsilon} + \frac{\phi C_i'}{P}$$

of which the left hand side is the Lerner index of firm i; $r_i = q_i/(Q^l + Q^b)$ is firm i's market share; and

$$\epsilon = - \frac{P}{P'(Q^l + Q^b)}$$

is the elasticity of demand.

The Lerner index is positive from the equation, so the Cournot equilibrium of the black market is not socially efficient. The term r_i/ϵ represents the social cost due to incomplete competition; and $\phi C_i'/P$ represents the rent-seeking cost.

Figure 3.6 shows the deadweight loss in a suppressed market with black market production, where $C(.)$ is the sectoral production cost, and $C(Q^b + Q^l) - C(Q^l) = \sum C_i(q_i)$; Q^l is the supply on the official market, and satisfies $C'(Q^l) - p^l = 0$; Q^b is the black market supply, and satisfies $(1+\phi) C'(Q^b + Q^l) - P(Q^b + Q^l) = 0$; $p^m \equiv P(Q^l)$; and $p^b \equiv P(Q^l + Q^b)$. The supply on the black market is assumed to be competitive thus $r_i \approx 0 \; \forall \; i$. Area "a" is the direct deadweight loss due to the price control; area "b" is the deadweight loss due to rent-seeking. The total deadweight loss to society is

$$DWL^b = \int\limits_{Q^l}^{Q^b+Q^l} (1+\phi)C'(x)dx - \int\limits_{Q^l}^{Q^b+Q^l} C'(x)dx + \int\limits_{Q^b+Q^l}^{Q^*} P(x)dx - \int\limits_{Q^b+Q^l}^{Q^*} C'(x)dx$$

$$= \phi[C(Q^b+Q^l) - C(Q^l)] - C(Q^*) + C(Q^b+Q^l) + \int\limits_{Q^b+Q^l}^{Q^*} P(x)dx$$

where Q^* is the quantity supplied at the market equilibrium and satisfies $P(Q^*) - C'(Q^*) = 0$. Obviously, DWL^b is smaller than DWL^l, the direct deadweight loss without a black market.

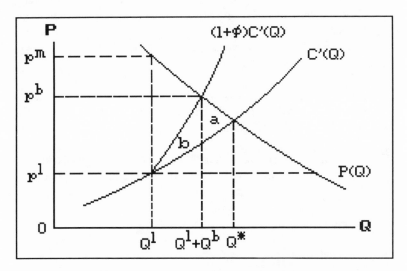

Figure 3.6 Deadweight Loss in a Suppressed Market with Black Market Transaction

NOTES

1. Baumol, W. 1990, op. cit.

2. Alm, James, "The Welfare Cost of the Underground Economy," *Economic Inquiry*, Vol. 23, no. 2, 1985, pp. 243-263.

3. Soto, Hernando de, *The Other Path: the Invisible Revolution in the Third World,* London: I. B. Tauris, 1989.

4. Marrese, M. op. cit.

5. Kantorovich, L.V., *The Best Use of Economic Resources,* Cambridge: Harvard University Press, 1965. Also, see Wellisz, S. and R. Findlay, "Central Planning and the 'Second Economy' in Soviet-Type Systems," *The Economic Journal*, Vol. 96, Sept.1986, pp. 646-658.

6. This is the rate that the consumption of one good must increase to compensate the utility loss due to the one-unit reduction of the consumption of the other good.

7. This is the rate that the production of one good must decrease to release resources to increase one unit of the production of the other good.

8. See Fung, op. cit.

9. Schumpeter, op. cit.

10. Kirzner, op. cit.

11. Marrese, M. op. cit.

12. Levine, H.S., "On the Nature and Location of Entrepreneurial Activity in Centrally Planned Economies: The Soviet Case" in *Entrepreneurship,* Joshua Ronen ed., Lexington, MA: Lexington Books, 1983, pp. 235-267.

13. Murphy, K. M., A. Shleifer, and R. W. Vishny, "Why is Rent-Seeking So Costly to Growth?" *AEA Papers and Proceedings*, May 1993, pp. 409-414.

14. Posner, R., "The Social Costs of Monopoly and Regulation," *Journal of Political Economy*, Vol. 83, 1975, pp. 807-827.

15. See Panico, Joseph A., *Queuing Theory: a Study of Waiting Lines for Business, Economics, and Science*, Englewood Cliffs, New Jersey: Prentice-Hall Inc., 1969, pp. 53-4 for a definition of this kind of queing problem.

16. Fisher, F., "The Social Costs of Monopoly and Regulations: Posner Reconsidered," *Journal of Political Economy*, Vol. 93, 1985, pp. 410-416. Tirole, J., *The Theory of Industrial Organization*, Cambridge, MA.: The MIT Press, 1988, pp. 76-77.

17. This case of bribery transfers is partly based on the model in Hillman, A. and E. Katz, "Hierarchical Structure and the Social Cost of Bribes and Transfers," *Journal of Public Economics*. Vol. 34, 1987, pp. 129-142.

18. In the conference "Hong Kong and Greater China" (October 1993), Gregory Chow argued that corruption is not necessarily a bad thing. His point is that corruption might improve economic efficiency and lead capital flow into most profitable industry. "In Mao's time, no corruption, no economic progress. In this market economy time, there is corruption, there is progress, more corruption, more progress." (*Chinese Community Forum* (CCF) [a journal published on China-Net], No. 9314, November 11, 1993).

19. Panico, Joseph A. op. cit.

20. For simplicity, the efficient-rationing rule is applied here and arbitrage between consumers is assumed to be frictionless.

CHAPTER 4

THE WANING PRIVATE BUSINESS OF THE 1950S

4.1 Introduction

This chapter reviews China's Socialist Transformation in the 1950s. During this stage, the government systematically implemented a program to suppress the operation of the market economy and to transform the economy into a centrally-planned one. The Socialist Transformation in China, however, differs significantly from the 1917 Russia (Soviet) Revolution led by Lenin and his Party. The Chinese communists did not follow the Soviet lead to nationalize the entire capitalist economy and replace private entrepreneurs with bureaucrats immediately after they came to power. Instead, they designed a step-by-step procedure to utilize, restrict, and transform the latter presumably in "a fairly long period of time." There was a period in the 1950s when the capitalist sector coexisted with the centrally-planned state sector. The Communist government, however, accelerated the transformation a few years later. The coexistence ended with an abrupt elimination of the capitalist sector in 1956-57. Besides political and ideological reasons, there seems to be an economic rationale behind the policy change: the corruption of private entrepreneurship and the declining productivity of the private sector in suppressed markets.

Section 4.2 introduces the official guidelines for the transformation. Section 4.3 describes how the government drew private business into the orbit of state planning by developing the "state capitalism." Section 4.4 discusses how private enterprises lost their competitive edge and innovative dynamics when their business opportunities and profits became subject to bureaucratic decisions. In Section 4.5, the government's decision to abolish the "state capitalism" was examined with respect to the growth of rent-seeking activity of private businesspeople. Section 4.6 concludes the discussion.

4.2 The Socialist Transformation

As early as in the 1920s, when the Chinese Communist Party was fighting a guerrilla war against the Nationalist government, it named its controled area in Jiangxi Province "The Soviet Republic of China." When the Chinese Communist Party took power in 1949, it aspired to build China into a socialist, industrialized country, according to the Soviet blueprint. This long term goal called for the transformation of the entire economy from a basically private and market-oriented economy into a centrally-planned one. In the transformed economy, all industrial enterprises and some agricultural farms would be owned and run by the state. Most of the agricultural labor would be organized into collective farms. No place was to be reserved for capitalist firms, not even for small private peddlers. China's Socialist Transformation, however, was a gradual program significantly different from the overnight elimination of the private sector during the 1917 Russia (Soviet) Revolution. China's Constitution of 1952 stated the *General Line for the Transition Period*: "Between the founding of the People's Republic of China and the erection of the socialist society lies a transitional period, in which the main task of the state is the gradual socialist transformation of agriculture, handicrafts as well as capitalist industry and capitalist trade."[1] This statement was the guideline for the Socialist Transformation. It set an agenda for a gradual and systematic transformation of the private economy.

The private economy in China before the Socialist Transformation consisted of three categories of participants: household peasants; capitalists; small merchants (peddlers) and handicraftsmen. The government designed a step-by-step procedure to transform these elements of the private economy.[2]

For agricultural peasants, the first step was to organize them into mutual aid teams. In a mutual aid team, several financially independent peasant households worked collectively in order to attain some degree of economies of scale. When mutual aid teams evolved from seasonal ones to all-year around ones, a higher form of collective organization, the "elementary agricultural producers' cooperative" at the village level, was to be established. In an elementary cooperative, private ownership of land and other means of production remained as a pooling of shares while farmers worked under a unified management to accomplish the advantage of division of labor. The next step of collectivization was the creation of the "advanced agricultural producers' cooperative." In the advanced cooperative, ownership of the means of production was transferred from private to collective and a farmer's income was solely determined by his/her working performance. The final step of this procedure was to transfer the ownership of advanced cooperatives to the state and to convert collective farms to state farms.

For capitalist enterprises, the first step was the development of the "elementary state capitalism," which meant a contract-relation between the state and private enterprises for processing orders (a more detailed explanation will be given below). The next was the "advanced state capitalism," in which the capitalists in joint state-private enterprises received fixed dividends from the enterprise and had only nominal voice in management. The final step was to turn these joint enterprises into fully state-owned enterprises.

For handicraftsmen and peddlers, the first step was to form "supply and marketing groups." Some of these groups functioned to purchase raw materials from and sell products to state commercial establishments. Others acted as retail distribution agents for the state wholesalers or received orders for processing goods. The second step was to set up the "supply and marketing cooperatives." In these cooperatives, production began to be organized under unified management but private ownership of tools and equipment was to be retained. The next step would organize the handicraftsmen or peddlers' cooperatives. The establishment of these cooperatives would transfer the ownership of tools and equipment from the private hands to the cooperative. Finally, in the long term, these cooperatives would convert to state-owned handicraft or commercial enterprises and factories.

Generally, the government would apply pressure and guidance to transform these elements of the private economy from private, to collective-private, then semi-socialist, and finally fully-fledged socialist economies. In non-agricultural sectors, the capitalist enterprises were the main targets of socialist transformation.

4.3 The Capitalists in a Socialist Command Economy

A gradual suppression of free markets characterized the entire procedure of the Socialist Transformation. To capitalist enterprises, the government adopted a packet policy of "utilization, restriction, and transformation," which was stipulated in Article 10 of the 1954 Constitution of the People's Republic of China.[3] This policy aimed to utilize the capitalist economy for rehabilitation of the national economy and then step by step restructure it into the state-owned economy by restricting its free development. Until the end of the Socialist Transformation, the capitalist sector coexisted with the centrally-planned socialist sector. During this stage, the suppression of free markets altered the nature of private entrepreneurship.

The government policy during the Utilization Stage (1949 to 1952) aimed to fight against "speculative" activity while aiding the development of "normal" private business. The purpose of the policy was to draw private business into the orbit of state planning and restrict to a minimum any spontaneous market allocation that conflicted with the priorities of central planning.

In its "Decision on Unifying National Finance and Economy" of March 1953, the government vowed to unify the nation's finance, material supply, and cash management under its control.[4] The government's first step was to shut down financial and capital markets in the name of fighting against financial speculation. This included the sudden shutdown of the Shanghai Stock Exchange, the largest stock exchange market in the Far East, in June 1949.[5] Next, the government nationalized private financial institutions. Before the Communist Party came to power, most private enterprises relied on private banks for the funding of short-term and long-term investment. In 1950, the government first centralized all government financial resources in the state banks, forcing many private banks to cease operation. It then mandatorily demanded commercial banks to increase their capitalization, forcing more private banks out of business. Finally, the government ordered the merge of the remaining private institutions into five major banking groups and put these banking groups under the supervision of government-directed administrative boards. With these measures, the state banks controlled more than 90 percent of the nation's bank deposits and loans.[6] By the end of 1952, the private banking system was eliminated in China.[7]

The drying up of financial markets forced private industry into a recession in early 1950.[8] The government responded by "readjusting" the relationship between the state and the private sector.[9] The state began to stimulate private enterprises by placing processing orders with them. This measure made private enterprises process goods for the state. The government organs also appointed private firms as retail distributors or commission agents of the state. In this way, private enterprises obtained raw materials and business opportunities. They also earned a certain amount of profit from their sale to the state. The government called this arrangement the "elementary state capitalism." Besides accepting government processing orders, private enterprises were still free to operate for the market and to do business in response to market signals. Besides feeding capitalist enterprises with processing contracts and raw materials, the state also started to restrict the private sector by intervening in the operation of private business. The *Provisional Regulations for Private Enterprises* of December 1950 stipulated in detail the conditions under which private firms were allowed to operate. It required private enterprises to submit their complete plans of production and sales for state approval. It also outlined the proportional distribution of private business earnings among dividends, welfare funds, taxes, and reserve funds.[10]

Following the start of the Korean War, the state placed enormous orders for military supplies with the private sector. The private economy not only revived but also expanded in this period, recording the year 1951 as the "golden year" of Chinese capitalists under the Communist Government.[11] From 1949 to 1952, the gross product value of the private industrial sector increased 54.2 percent, and that of the joint state-private enterprise increased more than five times.[12] The policy of utilization was a successful tactic of the Communist Party to exploit Chinese capitalists for three reasons. First, the capitalist firms provided an important source of budget revenue for the state. From 1950 to 1951, about one third of the state budget revenue came from the taxes paid and government bonds purchased by private industrial and commercial enterprises.[13] Second, the processing contracts not only ensured a large amount of military supplies for the war, but also enabled the state to obtain important industrial products. The government used these products to build a unified national material supply system under central planning. In 1950, the state started to put the supply of grain, industrial equipment, and important raw materials under its control.[14] In the first two years of the 1950s, the state widely set up "supply and marketing cooperatives" in the rural area with one hand and provided processing contracts to private industrial enterprises with the other. By doing so, the state-owned commercial institutions replaced private wholesale dealers as the major intermediary between the industrial sector and the agricultural sector. By 1952, beyond the noncommercial material supply within the state-owned sector, more than 60 percent of domestic wholesale trade was under the control of state commercial institutions.[15] Third, the rapid revival and growth of the private sector also gained the confidence of many leading industrialists, who had previously withdrawn their capital from China and now returned.[16]

4.4 The Transformed Nature of Private Entrepreneurs

Chinese capitalists were well known as hardworking, innovative, and shrewd entrepreneurs before the Communist revolution. This image, however, drastically changed in the 1950s when the new government drew capitalist firms into the orbit of a planned economy. As shown in Figure 4.1, government-assigned processing orders became the major business opportunity for the private sector in the early 1950s. This development, along with other restrictions imposed on private enterprises, encouraged entrepreneurs to engage in rent-seeking activities, which in turn caused social problems.

First, since a firm's profitability was mainly determined by the chance to receive government-assigned processing orders, the business community found it less worthwhile to conduct profit seeking by creating or searching for new products and new markets. It now became lucrative to obtain processing orders by toadying to government officials in charge.

Second, under the processing orders placed by the government, the profit for business owners was included in processing charges and the price of the products, and calculated in terms of cost. Therefore, businesspeople had less incentive than they would in a free market economy to reduce production cost. They sometimes even raised the cost purposely by wasting raw materials and paying unwarranted higher wages.[17] For example, in 1952, to produce one spindle of cotton yarn, private factories in Shanghai used about four more kilograms of cotton than their state-run counterparts. Similar problems were found in other industries, too.[18]

Third, administrative distribution had largely replaced the market allocation of capital and raw materials. This system concentrated formidable economic rents in the hands of those government officials who are in charge of the distribution of raw materials and production funds to the private enterprises. For most private entrepreneurs, bribing these officials to seek these rents became an irresistible temptation.

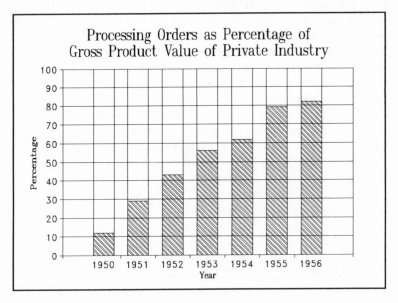

Figure 4.1
Source: Xue, Su, and Lin, *The Socialist Transformation of China's National Economy,* Beijing, China: People's Press, 1964, p. 117.

Fourth, because government control of material flow became so important, its impact on market transactions could decide the fortunes of private speculators. Therefore, obtaining inside economic information from related government officials became critical to business success.

Fifth, during the period, the communist regime never tried to develop a legal framework to define and protect private property rights during the 1950s. With such a background, the state and the private sector were likely to get involved in business disputes concerning property rights. This made it easier for private businesspeople to take advantage of the situation as well as for government officials to accuse private business of stealing public property.

Sixth, the government regulation and monitoring toward private firms became increasingly restrictive. Businesspeople sought to escape the controls by bribing the official in charge.

The coexistence of a state planned economy and a private economy in the utilization stage therefore provided many opportunities for rent-seeking entrepreneurship. The government labeled some rent-seeking activities of capitalists as the "five evils": bribery of government staff, tax evasion, theft of state property, cheating on government contracts, and stealing of economic information for speculative purposes. Capitalists were accused of having "tried by every possible means to break away from the leadership of the state-owned economy," "refused to accept orders for processing work" (when it is no longer profitable), and "resorted to various despicable methods to carry out illegal activities in order to rake in exorbitant profits."[19]

On the other hand, by the end of the utilization stage, corruption soon became a prevailing tendency, not only among some civil and military personnel of the KMT (Nationalist) regime who were taken over and now served the new government, but also among the cadres who had joined the communist revolution for years. For example, the head of China's secret police announced during the campaign against the corruption that 80 percent of the administrative personnel were corrupt in various degrees.[20] The government was alarmed by the rapid spread of the so-called "three evils" (corruption, waste, and bureaucratism) among its staff. As a government document pointed out, "Corruption and waste are the arch enemies of the movement to increase production and practice economy, and they have seriously impaired the interests of the state and the people. Unless this serious phenomenon is checked and overcome, it will corrode our newborn state organ."[21]

In 1951 the government launched the campaign against the "three evils" to purify its bureaucracy. The campaign exposed thousands of corruption scandals. Very soon the government turned to strike the private sector, which it saw as the root of bureaucratic corruption. In 1952 the government started the campaign against the "five evils."[22] The Party mobilized millions of workers to denounce their employers. Among 450,000 private enterprises in the eight major cities, 76 percent were accused of committing illegal transactions and ordered to pay large fines. Much of the capitalists' profit made by the private business during the Korean War was confiscated. Most private enterprises' working capital was drained.[23] It was during this campaign that all the private banks incurred severe losses and the state adopted prompt measures to turn them into joint state-private banks, which in fact became agencies of the state bank.

The campaign brought China's capitalism into the Restriction Stage (1952 to 1953). In 1953 the government took systematic measures to restrict the activities of private wholesale dealers. Through planned and compulsory purchase in the rural area, government agencies enforced unified control over wholesale trade, especially the trade of major agricultural raw materials. The government also introduced planned supply of coal, iron, steel, and other important industrial materials. Thus, the state-owned and cooperative commercial enterprises finally replaced the private wholesale dealers during this stage.[24]

For the industrial capitalists, the blow was heavy as well. To avoid a general recession of the manufacturing industry, the government "decided to allow a tiny number of major speculators and enterprises which were not beneficial but only harmful to society to go bankrupt, but adopted suitable measures to help private industrial and commercial undertakings carry on their business, because only in this way could the state collect taxes from them."[25] By receiving new processing and manufacturing orders from the government, most of the private industrial and commercial business survived the campaign, but became more closely woven into the central planning system. Private enterprises no longer operated with the freedom they had enjoyed during the Utilization Period. They started to lose financial and managerial independence under the closer supervision of government officials.

A number of enterprises, which found themselves owing the government a huge amount of fines after the campaign, were forced to be transformed into joint state-private enterprises. The state claimed a share of ownership of these enterprises and therefore assigned personnel to participate in management. In the Communist Party's terminology, this development marked the emergence of a new combination of capitalist business and socialist planning ——— the "advanced state capitalism."

4.5 Abolition of the "State Capitalism"

The above changes further stifled the private sector's productive (profit-seeking) entrepreneurship. After the autumn of 1953, the state had, within its policy framework of "planned purchase and supply," taken over the entire wholesale trade in important agricultural and industrial products.[26] By organizing the private retail traders as distributors for state commercial establishments, the government had virtually eliminated a freely competitive market. Without such a market, even private enterprises became less eager to improve or expand their business. This trend became increasingly obvious after the campaign against the "five evils." Before the eve of The Transformation Period (1954 to 1957), Chinese capitalist enterprises exhibited prevailing reluctance to innovate. Private enterprises were characterized with under-investment, great waste, poor-quality products, unnecessary inventories, stockpiling of raw materials, and other serious irregularities.[27] As the proportion of centrally planned resource allocation increased in industrial production, the private sector found it more difficult to maintain production due to the shortage of supply in raw materials. By the second half of 1954, private industries in major urban areas faced serious difficulties, with many private enterprises struggling on the verge of bankruptcy.[28] In contrast the joint state-private enterprises thrived at the supply of state funds and production plans. According to official sources, labor productivity in joint state-private enterprises was twice of that in private enterprises by 1955.[29]

After the restriction period, the government launched a new campaign of overall socialist transformation. The speed of transformation accelerated immediately. Figure 4.2. and 4.3 show the rapid change of ownership structure during the period. Within a few months from 1956 to 1957, the entire industry, commerce, and handicrafts were socialized or collectivized. Most of the capitalist enterprises were transformed into joint state-private enterprises.

Considered as "the higher form of state capitalism," the joint state-private enterprise stood nominally under the joint management of capitalists and the state representatives. The capitalists, however, had only a nominal voice in management. The assets of the private enterprises were turned into private shares. The government claimed its share of ownership based on its investment in these enterprises and the debt that capitalists owed. In the early 1950s, the dividends paid to the private share owners were limited to a quarter of industrial profits. Later from 1956 to 1957, joint state-private enterprises were reformed into the "highest form of state capitalism." The jargon refers to a joint state-private business group by the whole trade. It was in fact the state trust, which contained all the enterprises of the corresponding branches of an industry. Through this business organization, centrally planned production was supposed to be coordinated more efficiently. After the setup of the organization, in place of the previously paid dividends, capitalists began to receive an annual fixed interest of five percent on their capital for seven years. At the same time, these entrepreneurs were converted to salary-earning state employees.[30] This transformation severed the relationship between the capitalists' income and their business and finally buried the legal status of capitalist entrepreneurship.

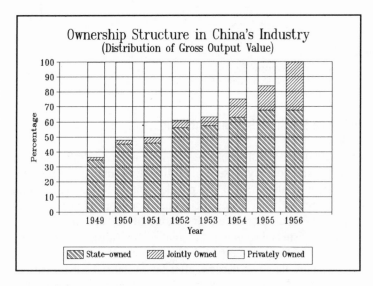

Figure 4.2

Source: State Statistical Bureau of the PRC, *Ten Great Years*, Beijing: Foreign Language Press, 1960, p. 38.

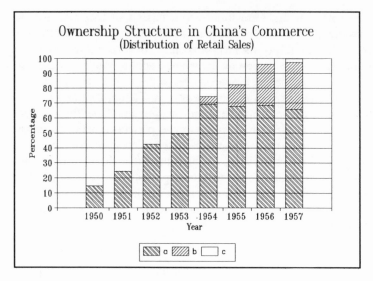

Figure 4.3
a —— State-owned Enterprises
b —— State-capitalist and Cooperative Enterprises
c —— Private Enterprises

Source: State Statistical Bureau of the PRC, op. cit., p. 40.

From 1950 to 1957, the Chinese government successfully absorbed the entire private economy of several million firms and tens of millions of independent handicraftsmen and peddlers into a Soviet-type central planning system without causing social unrest or economic chaos. This peaceful transformation marked the result of an effective mix of ideological idealism and economic pragmatism by Chinese communists. The socialist transformation established a nationwide centrally-planned system. For more than two decades after the Socialist Transformation, Chinese capitalists ceased to exist as a class and the role of the private sector became almost negligible in the national economy.

4.6 Concluding Comments

In the 1950s, China's practice of drawing private enterprises into the orbit of a centrally-planned system corrupted the nature of private entrepreneurship as well as government bureaucrats. Private entrepreneurs lost their competitive edge and innovative dynamics, while many government bureaucrats indulged in abusing administrative power for bribes. These facts are consistent with the theoretical results in the previous chapters: In distorted markets contrived benefits provok rent seeking, which directs entrepreneurial resources from productive uses to unproductive uses. The market suppression subjects firms' profitability to rent-seeking influence. The economy is therefore trapped in a rent-seeking equilibrium that undermines economic efficiency.

It is worthwhile to note that the sudden speedup of the Socialist Transformation in 1956 was not implemented according to the Party's earlier agenda. At first, a Communist Party's Central Committee meeting in 1952 proposed that the whole process of the Socialist Transformation should take "a fairly long period of time." This was consistent with Mao Zedong's claim in 1947 that since the Chinese economy was so backward "even after the country-wide victory of the revolution, it will still be necessary to permit the existence for a long time of a capitalist sector of the economy."[31] Later, the First National People's Congress held in 1954 defined the schedule of the Socialist Transformation to be fifteen years.[32] Only three years after that announcement, however, the Party and the government implemented drastic institutional changes that eliminated China's capitalist economy and entirely collectivized the agricultural and handicraft sectors.

Most researchers on the issue attribute the speedup of the Transformation to ideological and political reasons. Our analysis in this chapter shows, besides ideological-political reasons, there was some economic rationality behind the action as far as capitalist enterprises were concerned. To the government, the main benefit of maintaining the capitalist sector lay in the utilization of the latter's productive capacity, managerial skills, and financial resources. Under the so-called "elementary state capitalism," however, capitalist entrepreneurs exhibited diminishing interest and capability in improving productivity. Their shrewdness no longer contributed actively to economic growth, but to a variety of rent-seeking activities. These activities grew to a threat to the order of centrally-planned economy and the efficiency of its bureaucratic apparatus. From the government's perspectives, the negative aspects of the "elementary state capitalism" appeared to outweigh its beneficial ones. Therefore, the government switched gears to abandon the "state-capitalism" without delay, hoping to attain better efficiency in a centrally-planned economy built solely on the state-owned and cooperative sectors.

NOTES

1. Cited according to Kraus, Willy, *Economic Development and Social Change in the People's Republic of China*. New York: Springer-Verlag, 1982, p. 51.

2. The policies regarding the step-by-step transformation were summarized in Xue Muqiao, Su Xing, and Lin Zili, *Zhongguo Guomin Jingji de Shehui Zhuyi Gaizao* (The Socialist Transformation of China's National Economy), Beijing, China: People's Press, 1964.

3. *The Constitution of the People's Republic of China*. Beijing, China: Foreign Languages Press, 1954, p. 76.

4. Yang Jianbai, *Zhonghua Renmin Gongheguo Guomin Jingji Huifu he Fazhan de Chengjiu* (The Success of Rehabilitating and Developing the National Economy in the P.R. China). Beijing, China: Statistical Press, 1956, p. 21.

5. Liu and Wu ed. op. cit., p. 26.

6. Xue, Su, and Lin, op. cit., p. 29.

7. See *China's Economic Development: Growth and Structural Change* [Cheng, Chu-yuan. Boulder, Colorado: Westview Press, 1982] pp. 140-142 for a more detailed account of the nationalization of private financial institutions.

8. Xue, Su, and Lin, op. cit., p. 29.

9. See Liu and Wu ed., op. cit. pp. 41-44 for a detail account of the policies to adjust the relationship between the state and the capitalist sector.

10. Cheng, op. cit., p. 144

11. See Liu and Wu ed., op. cit., pp. 45-46 for an account of the booming of private business in industry, commerce, and transportation in the period.

12. Yang Jianbai, op. cit., p. 49.

13. Xu Dixin, *Zhongguo Guodu Shiqi Guomin Jingji Fenxi* (An Analysis on China's National Economy in the Transformation Period: 1946-57). Beijing, China: People's Press, 1962, p. 196.

14. Yang Jianbai, op. cit., p. 21.

15. Xu Dixin, op. cit., p. 171.

16. See New China News Agency's report about the development, *Renmin Ribao* (People's Daily), 18 September 1952, p. 3.

17. Xue, Su, Lin, op. cit. p. 125; Cheng, op. cit. p. 148.

18. Xu Dixin, op. cit. p. 108.

19. Liu and Wu ed., op. cit., p. 67.

20. *Renmin Ribao* (People's Daily), 17 Jan. 1952, p. 1.

21. "The National Committee of the Chinese People's Political Consultative Conference: The Directive of December 29, 1951," (Liu and Wu ed., op. cit., appendix, p. 520).

22. Chinese Academy of Social Sciences, *Zhongguo Zibenzhuyi Gongshangye de Shehuizhuyi Gaizao* (Socialist Transformation of Capitalist Industry and Commerce in China). Beijing: People's Press, 1978, pp. 77-85.

23. Cheng, op. cit., pp. 144-145, Xue, Su, and Lin, op. cit., p. 33.

24. Chinese Academy of Social Sciences, op. cit., pp. 88-89.

25. Liu and Wu ed., op. cit., p. 69.

26. Xue, Su, and Lin, op. cit., p. 118.

27. Almanac Editorial Board, *Zhongguo Jingji Nianjian* (Almanac of China's Economy). Beijing: Publisher of Beijing Journal of Economic

Management, 1981, Part V, p. 121; also see Cheng op. cit., p. 148.

28. Liu and Wu ed., op. cit., p. 141.

29. Xue, Su, and Lin, op. cit., p. 130.

30. Xue, Su, and Lin, op. cit., pp. 134-35.

31. Mao Zedong, *Selected Works of Mao Zedong*, 4 vols, Beijing, China: Foreign Language Press, 1966, Vol. 4, p. 168.

32. Liu and Wu ed., op. cit., p. 114.

CHAPTER 5

THE STRUGGLE FOR SURVIVAL IN THE MAO ERA

5.1 Introduction

The Socialist Transformation was supposed to prepare China's economy for a Soviet-type centrally-planned economy. Mao Zedong and other Chinese Communist leaders, however, were not content with following the course of the Stalinist model. Immediately after the completion of the Socialist Transformation, the Communist leaders started to experiment with Mao's own ideas of socialism as in the form of the Great Leap Forward. During the two decades between the completion of the Socialist Transformation and the ejection of Mao's selected heir Hua Guofeng, Chinese Communist elites vacillated between Mao's utopian economic romance and the pragmatic policies of some non-Maoist leaders.[1] The power struggles among the top leaders had profound impact upon the institutional setting of the remnant private economy in China. This chapter assesses the impact and examines the development of the private sector, the semi-private sector, and the underground economy during this period.

Section 5.2 introduces the ideological background of government policy making in the Mao era. Section 5.3 describes how non-planned production and trade developed because of political instability and local empire building. Section 5.4 and Section 5.5 show the changing environment of the private sector in rural and urban areas. The development of the underground economy is discussed in Section 5.6. Section 5.7 summarizes the characteristics of entrepreneurial activity in the Mao era.

5.2 Ideology v.s. Pragmatism

In the Chinese Communist Party, both the Maoists and non-Maoists leaders held Marxist-Leninist view that socialism was the first stage of the communist society. Public ownership and central planning were the two major characteristics of the socialist state. The differences between the two factions lay in the blueprint for the socialist economy and the procedures necessary in structuring a communist society. Mao developed his own socialist theory and attempted to remould China according to his theory. Some non-Maoist leaders, however, as pragmatists rather than ideologists, did not have a comprehensive conceptual thought about socialism that was comparable to Mao's.[2] The basic controversial issues between Mao's economic thoughts of socialism and the non-Maoist alternatives can be summarized as follows:

Politics and economic development.
Mao believed that class conflicts were permanent in a socialist society. Even after the capitalist class was eliminated, bourgeois influence would remain because there was a spontaneous tendency toward capitalism among the peasants and small private producers ("the petty bourgeois"). The Party should therefore keep alert to the possibility that capitalism could be reasserted and it should put political work in charge of economic development and carry out the "continuous revolution under the proletarian dictatorship."[3] This revolution would free the forces of production blocked by the rigidity of production relations and therefore would be the major source of economic development.

In contrast, Liu Shao-qi[4] and other non-Maoist leaders viewed the end of the Socialist Transformation as the termination of major class struggles. Therefore, economic construction should become the major task of the Communist Party. In his political report on the Eighth National Congress of the CPC, Liu Shao-qi stressed that the period of class struggle was over and the major task confronting the Party was economic development.[5] Only when society's productivity developed to an advanced level could further innovation of production relations be beneficial.

Economic organization.

The essence of Mao's economic thought embodies his idea of a society composed of the people who were selfless and devoted to the cause of communism. These people would possess the capacity for total self-denial and would wholeheartedly and willingly sacrifice their individual interests for the goal of revolution. Such people exemplify Mao's concept of a "communist man."[6] To build a society like this, Mao resorted to implanting communist ideology into individuals' minds through several measures. One was the continuous criticism of individualism. Another measure was to organize self-sufficient communes with very little division of labor and with an egalitarian distribution of income. His first attempt was to set up the quasi-military "people's commune" in the period of the Great Leap Forward (1958 to 1959). The early forms of the people's commune were organized along military lines. The members lived the collective way and worked like soldiers fighting a battle. Nearly all forms of private property were banned and even the function of the family was reduced to a minimum.[7] After the first people's commune was set up in 1958, Mao commented:

"It is good to set up people's communes. Their advantage is that they combine industry, agriculture, commerce, education and military affairs, thus making the task of leadership easier."[8]

Mao viewed the people's commune as a fundamental way to eradicate the "three basic differences" that caused inequality, namely, the difference existed between workers and peasants, the one existed between urban and rural areas, and the one existed between mental labor and manual labor. In the high tide of Great Leap Forward, urban communes also emerged in some major cities.[9]

Even after the failure of the Great Leap Forward, Mao never relinquished his search for a feasible organization that would approach his ideal of a society with a minimum division of labor and a minimum disparity in wealth. In 1964 he proclaimed the slogans, "In agriculture learn from Dazhai" and "In industry learn from Daqing," to support his model of economic organization. Dazhai was a village production brigade in northern Shanxi Province. Daqing was an oil-field administrative bureau in northeastern China. Dazhai and Daqing shared some similar management characteristics: Nonmaterial incentives linked to communist morality, semi-military discipline, egalitarian income distribution, frugality of members' lives, and reliance upon revolutionary fervor to achieve progress in productivity.[10] At the beginning of the Cultural Revolution, Mao proposed his blueprint of economic organization in his well-known May 7 Instruction. In this instruction, he advocated that workers, peasants, soldiers, and students should merge the activities of industrial production, agricultural and subsidiary production, military training, political campaigns, and studies in a quasi-military organization.[11]

Mao also favored local autonomy and self-reliance. This was partially due to his design of economic organization and his contempt of the division of labor. His estimate of the international situation in the 1960s also made him believe that the risk of a large-scale war was imminent and therefore China should diffuse its industries to the local level. Mao said:

> "Local administrations must do whatever is necessary to establish autonomous industrial systems: this would first consist of cooperative regions, then extend to several provinces." [12]

Based on his views of mass mobilization and local autonomy, Mao advocated the policy of "walking on two legs," which means that the rural development of local small industries based on simple technology should go in parallel with the development of large and medium-sized modern plants in urban areas. All provinces were encouraged to build themselves into small but complete industrial systems. These systems should be fairly self-sufficient in the production of raw materials, machinery, and consumer goods.[13]

Contrary to Mao's model of economic organization, the non-Maoist leaders like Liu Shao-qi and Chen Yun appeared to prefer a centralized planning apparatus. They believed that the apparatus would serve the purpose of building a modern industrialized economy with a high degree of division of labor and specialization.[14] Consequently, whenever the non-Maoist leaders were in charge of economic affairs, they tended to strengthen central planning and to fabricate regulations for administering economic activities according to modern managerial principles.

Economic romance.

With his experience in guerrilla warfare and his conception of the "communist man," Mao developed a belief in mass mobilization in economic construction. He thought that reliance on human willpower could break the routine of economic development and create miracles.[15]

He claimed that "We cannot trail behind other countries, following the beaten path"[16] in achieving economic development. During the Mao era, the official propaganda promoted nonmaterial incentives with an emphasis on the role of political consciousness and the repudiation of private material rewards. Whenever Maoists were in charge, any material incentive scheme or reward system that might undermine equality was seen as capitalist and was repeatedly under attack for favoring the "bourgeois rights" or "economism."[17] Therefore the systems of the bonus reward, piece rate payroll, and even the eight-grade wage scale in state-owned industries were under criticism in the Great Leap Forward and the Cultural Revolution. In this atmosphere, the regime kept to a low-wage policy throughout the early 1960s until Mao's death in 1976.[18] Mao's overwhelming stress on human willpower and mass mobilization made him despise the role of professional expertise. He publicly protested his disbelief in the modern management and strict planning apparatus.[19]

In the non-Maoist leaders' view, industrialization involved complicated modern technology and management. Centrally-planned economic development required the careful calculation of resource allocation administered by experts. Therefore, they placed their reliance on bureaucratic specialists and the central planning apparatus rather than on mass mobilization. In addition, the non-Maoists also emphasized the role of material incentives in achieving economic progress. Since they considered the market and the private economy as supplementary to the centrally-planned economy, they tended to adopt a pragmatic attitude toward the private economic activities.[20]

5.3 The Growth of Cellular Economy

The political struggles among the top leaders led to drastic wavering in government policy, which in turn produced frequent economic instability. The control of economic policy making switched hands several times between the two factions. Maoist ideology dominated economic affairs in the periods of the Great Leap Forward and the Cultural Revolution. The pragmatic leaders were in control during the "retrenchment and adjustment years" after the Great Leap Forward and for a brief period in the Cultural Revolution. These changes frequently impeded the process of national planning. Therefore, a highly centralized command system never operated normally during the Mao era. Localities and their enterprises, at the same time, gained significant autonomy over production and trade decisions. Consequently, the non-planned production and trade arena was open to widespread "empire building" among the localities and production units. Some effects of the power struggle are as follows.

The damages to the planning apparatus.

One of the most important prerequisites for a centrally planned economy was its information collecting apparatus. The building of China's nationwide statistical agency network was started during the First Five Year Plan period (1953 to 1957).[21] This work was interrupted, however, by the Great Leap Forward in 1958. In the time the urgent political task of mass mobilization replaced the normal function of data collecting and analysis. Many statistical agencies were abolished and their staff members were transferred to other jobs. In the early 1960s, after the failure of the Great Leap Forward, the government re-instituted a vertical control system over statistical agencies. However, the Cultural Revolution once again disrupted the control system in the late 1960s and paralyzed the statistical apparatus for years. Falsification of statistics was widespread during those years.[22]

The number and size of the central planning and economic administrative organs met with the same fate as the statistical agencies. The political shocks severely curtailed their number and size. These organs' power and influence ebbed during the Great Leap Forward and the Cultural Revolution. Simultaneously, the number of ministries in charge of a single industry fluctuated almost constantly because of mergers, regroupings, and divisions over the years.[23] During the chaotic years from 1967 to 1969, most of the bureaucrats in charge of planning and economic administration were purged and the planning administrative organs even ceased to operate for months.[24] Also, a great majority of the Party cadres were forced to submit to "reeducation" through manual work in the late 1960s up to the early 1970s. After years of purges against experts and professionals, most of those who remained in charge of planning and economic administration by the end of the Mao era lacked necessary training in planning and management. An official survey revealed that in some provinces in 1980, none of the leaders on the prefectural and county levels were university or college graduates. Only a few leaders at those levels were capable of handling scientific, technical, or managerial matters.[25]

The growth of local cellular economies and the weakening of central control.

When China built its system of centralized economic planning in the First Five Year Plan period, the system was an almost mechanistic adoption of the Soviet model. It embodied all the features of over-centralized vertical ministry control and a detailed commanding administration.[26] The vertical hierarchy of central ministries was responsible for the absence of horizontal coordination of economic plans at the regional level.[27] Initiated by Mao, the government began in 1957 to direct the first decentralization reforms to "arouse the enthusiasm of the regions." These reforms empowered the provinces to set up regional economic plans encompassing all enterprises in their area of responsibility.[28] The system of vertical organization by branches of industries was complemented by a system of regional organization. By June 1958, nearly all manufacturers of consumer goods were under the control of major local authorities supervised by several central ministries, rather than directly by the Ministry of Light Industry in a Soviet model.[29]

The purpose of the 1957 reforms was to improve national planning by rationalizing the center-local relationship. The decentralization, however, was partially responsible for the rampant development of the "people's communes" in the climax of the Great Leap Forward. The Party decided to adopt the people's commune as "the basic unit of the social structure of our country" and "the basic organization of social power." Some leaders even began to talk about the "withering away of the state," exemplifying the realization of the old Marxist dream.[30] As a result, the share of the central government expenditure in total budget expenditures slid from the peak 73 percent in the First Five Year Plan period to 50.7 percent in 1959 and 43.7 percent in 1960.[31] The overheated mass mobilization at the local level and the inflated reports of achievements featured movement of the Great Leap Forward. These phenomena proved a diminution in the ability of the center to control the course of events or even to obtain correct information.

After the failure of the Great Leap Forward, the non-Maoist leaders immediately took a series of re-centralization measures to "correct the over-decentralization mistakes."[32] The share of the central government expenditure in total budget expenditures rose to 55 percent in the years from 1963 to 1966.[33] The Cultural Revolution, however, brought another chance for the provinces to gain influence in the planning of local production and the control of local investment capital.

From 1969 to 1970, reflecting Mao's favor for local autonomy and self-reliance and his perception of national security needs, the central government decided to put all enterprises "suitable for local management" under the control of local authorities. The central ministries only retained direct control over the key national enterprises and undertakings. By the end of 1970, the nine ministries under the central government in charge of industries and communications had transferred 2,237 of their 3,082 enterprises and undertakings to the local authorities.[34] This decision had a profound impact on China's planning and power structure. For instance, in 1973, the State Planning Commission drafted a ten-clause provision in an attempt to re-centralize some planning powers concerning capital construction, total employment and payroll, distribution of main materials and financial funds, and production plans. It did not succeed, however, in reversing the general decentralization tendency generated by the change in 1970.[35]

The development of non-planned production and trade.

The damage to the planning apparatus and the country's tendency toward geographic autarky left China's economy in a semi-planned and semi-anarchistic state during most years of the Cultural Revolution. Consequently, the growth of non-planned production and trade occurred at the local level. The non-planned production and trade at the local level were generally not regarded as private economic activity in the Mao era. This development, however, created elementary markets within the national planned economy and provided potential opportunities for entrepreneurial ventures. The non-planned production and trade became the basis for an underground private economy and a hotbed of bureaucratic corruption, exchange of favors for private interests, and other illegal activities.

Non-planned production at the local level was first observed in the late 1950s. During the Great Leap Forward, many small locally-controlled labor-intensive enterprises, especially the backyard furnace workshops, emerged nationwide in a national drive to develop steel and other heavy industries at the local level.[36] This temporary upsurge of local small industries was reversed later, however, as the government closed down thousands of these enterprises in the retrenchment and readjustment period of the early 1960s.

Non-planned production and trade revived and grew again in the years of the Cultural Revolution. Political chaos from 1967 to 1968 led to a severe shortage of raw materials. Many factories and mines were forced to cease production. Their equipment was left idle and transportation temporarily halted.[37] The shortage kept growing as central planning and coordination of material allocation weakened. The decentralization of the period from 1969 to 1970 had severed the centrally-planned allocation channels that had previously existed. As many enterprises were put under the dual leadership of ministries and localities, the coordination between the center and the local authorities became more complicated. Quite a few big enterprises transferred to the localities had to approach the central authorities for maintaining their nationwide supply and production links, and in this way found themselves now under multi-leadership of ministries and localities.[38] The abolition of the Ministry of Allocation of Materials and the localization of many enterprises left a vacancy of central control in the allocation of raw materials and capital goods.[39] Large industrial cities like Shanghai, which formerly relied upon central authorities to allocate the supply of raw materials from major steel and mining industrial bases, now found themselves left in a position of having to search for these supplies on their own efforts.[40]

This result had two effects: One was the prevalence of barter among localities beyond the direct control of central authorities. To fulfill the need that was not satisfied by the centrally-planned supply channels, many production units exchanged their products or controlled materials with other units without the approval of their superiors. The practice of dispatching purchasing agents to seek material supplies outside the centrally-planned supply channels therefore became an indispensable characteristic of Chinese enterprises during these years. An official report condemned this solution as an "unhealthy practice" that "has affected the fulfillment of the state production plan, undermined the Party's economic policy and socialist marketing."[41] The development of this quasi-market allocation of materials and capital equipment had a significant impact on the underground private economy. Individuals involved in these trades usually used informal market deals to exchange favors for their personal interests.

A second consequence that resulted from the lack of the central allocation of supplies was the development of autarkic planning at the local level. The localities competed for investment funds to build their local economic system in an attempt to reduce their reliance upon supplies from other regions, with no regard for nationwide comparative advantages. The "empire building" activity resulted in the redundant construction of projects that meant the generation of huge wastes. The economy was heading toward what A. Donnithorne has called a "cellular economy," which consists of many small, self-sufficient units operating without a unified national plan.[42]

Under Mao's theory of "walking on two legs" the development of five small local industries (iron and steel, machine-building, chemical fertilizer, coal mining, and cement) was encouraged by the central government. The state earmarked eight billion yuan from 1970 to 1975 as a special fund to support the provincial level localities to develop these small industries. Sixty percent of the profits made by the "five small industries" built and run by the county authorities would in the two to three years be kept by the county authorities.[43] In 1970, a vigorous development of small local enterprises in rural areas started. More than 90 percent of counties had built networks of small plants for these industries. Many projects were delegated to the commune or even production brigade level. As a result, in the early 1970s, China's rural commune and brigade industries developed to a sizeable non-planned sector.[44] These enterprises were nominally collectively owned by the commune or brigade, but were financially controlled by local county or township (commune) authorities. Usually the production of these enterprises was not subject to the unified state plan and central administration.[45] Because state plans did not include their needs for raw materials, fuels, market outlets, and transportation, these enterprises had to "grease someone's palms" to achieve their ends. They "resort to gifts, wining and dining, and briberies to scramble for their own raw material and market outlets," leading to corruption, waste, speculation, and manipulation.[46] In some areas, these enterprises gradually developed to cooperatives or even essentially private enterprises, becoming a hotbed for the private underground economic activities.

5.4 Private Business in the People's Commune

The official policy toward free markets and private production and trade was generally stern during the Mao era. However, political struggles caused frequent wavering in official policy. A barometer of the unstable policy was the official tolerance of peasants' private plots, their household sideline production, and the free market sale of their products.

In China, the government taxed peasants by imposing purchasing quota volumes on rural collectives. The state purchasing prices for these quota volumes, usually the list prices or sometimes the above-quota markup prices or the "negotiated prices," were generally lower than free market prices. Figure 5.1 shows changes of the list price index, the state purchasing price index, and the free market price index from 1952 to 1977.[47]

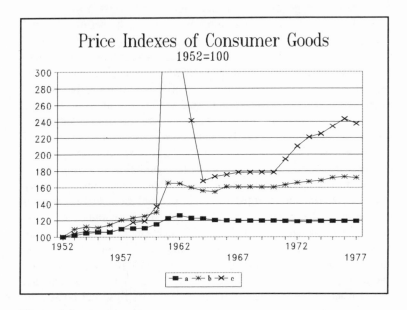

Figure 5.1

a——The List Price Index;

b——The State Purchasing Price Index;

c——The Free Market Price Index.

Note: The term "Consumer goods" in this statistics refers to a package of goods for subsistence, including grain, oil bearing crops, cotton, tobacco, hemp, meat, fowl, eggs, aquatic products, vegetables, fruits, firewood and grass, etc. Although the three indexes are set at 100 for the year 1952, the graph does NOT imply that these prices were actually equal in 1952. Therefore when the purchasing price index appears to be higher than the free market price index, the normal relations among the three prices may still hold. These relations are: The list prices are lower than the state purchasing prices and the state purchasing prices lower than free market prices.

Source: *China Trade and Price Statistics 1988*, New York: Praeger Publishers, 1989.

Since the state purchasing prices were kept well below free market prices during the Mao era, the collectives, as well as individual peasants, had a strong incentive to participate in free market trade.

When the Socialist Transformation was coming to a close in 1956, there was a brief period of relaxation. Chen Yun, who was then the minister of commerce, reintroduced free markets for sideline foodstuffs.[48] The policy applied free-market trading to the agricultural goods retained for peasants who have met planned purchase quotas. The free-market goods also included those agricultural products not covered by the plan. In addition, the government permitted small traders and peddlers to operate in towns and villages. The prices of non-rationed perishable goods and some other commodities were allowed to be determined by market demand and supply. Peasants also enjoyed a raise of the maximum size of private plots from five percent to ten percent of the average arable land per head in the collective.[49]

Very soon the Great Leap Forward and the establishment of people's communes abruptly interrupted this brief period of liberalization. The nationwide campaign of setting up people's communes started in 1958. Under the guideline to bring about ownership "by the whole people" via the people's commune, the Party and the government enlarged the scale of public ownership in rural areas from a village level to an average of 4,600 households. The scope of private ownership in rural areas shrunk sharply and all private ownership of the means of production, including the private plots and domestic animals disappeared. There is evidence that even the traditional family functions were reduced to a minimum during this period when public canteens, kindergartens, nurseries, and homes for the elder were set up in the commune. Consequently, the movement closed the rural farmers' markets.[50]

After the disastrous failure of the Great Leap Forward (1958 to 1960), the national economy was on the verge of collapse and thousands of peasants' lives were threatened by widespread famine.[51] The severe shortage of food led to soaring prices in the free market (see Figure 5.1). In the face of these difficulties, the government, operating under the influence of the non-Maoist leaders, again adopted a more pragmatic attitude toward the rural private economy. Along with a retreat in collectivization and a de facto dissolution of people's communes, the government returned to commune members the private plots and other personal properties confiscated at the beginning of the people's commune movement. The commune members were encouraged to engage in household sideline occupations and handicraft production (the plots were not to exceed seven percent of a production team's land).[52] Farmers' markets in rural areas revived in the fall of

1960, although they were under close regulation and monitor of on-the-spot supervisory officials. These markets enabled the individual peasants to sell their sideline products. In addition, the new policy allowed communes and production brigades to sell their agricultural goods after having fulfilled their state assigned compulsory sales. In the fall of 1961, some 40,000 rural markets were formed. These newly established markets handled 25 percent of total rural sales turnover.[53] Meanwhile, a number of farm fairs also emerged in the big and medium-sized cities. Additionally, the government encouraged peasants to use their spare time to develop private plots and sideline production and promised to exempt the produce of these plots from compulsory sales to the state. The implementation of these central policies varied among different regions. As Prybyla has pointed out, certain liberalization policies were never fully operational in practice; while other policies were expanded beyond the official guidelines in some regions. For instance, during the Cultural Revolution, some non-Maoist local leaders were accused of having maintained twenty to fifty percent of cultivated land as private plots.[54]

The policy shift after the Great Leap Forward toward free markets was a pragmatic and expedient measure rather than a fundamental change. Official documents still considered rural farmers' markets ideologically undesirable and institutionally inconsistent with the central plan. The policy makers saw the presence of rural markets as temporarily necessary since the state and cooperative trading organs had proved unable to match the demands of the populace in times of economic difficulty. In general, the revival of free markets occurred on a limited scale. The village fair trade in the countryside and the farm fairs in the cities were subject to overly rigid restrictions. It was explicitly stipulated that the fairs in the cities should be retail markets for sideline products (other than grain and edible oil) only. The sellers should only be farmers from the outskirts of urban areas, small peddlers licensed to transport over short distances, city dwellers selling household sideline products, and individual handicraftsmen selling miscellaneous handicraft articles. State trading organs were to make sure that only permitted goods were offered in free markets, and to see that the private traders followed price ceiling guidelines. Statistics from 14 big and medium-sized cities at the end of 1962 showed that the amount of trade at these fairs, calculated according to the list prices of state-owned enterprises, accounted for only two percent of the total retail sales of commodities.[55]

As the national economy gradually recovered from the manmade famine and disaster of the early 1960s, the government soon shifted its emphasis to the collective sideline production and again issued warnings about "the spontaneous capitalist tendencies" inherent in private sideline occupations. By 1963, in order to keep peasants working on planned collective production rather than devoting themselves to private production, the government imposed more restrictions on the rural fair trade and curtailed private peddling. It vowed to reduce the scope of the rural fair trade and gradually replace it with state-owned commercial undertakings and the supply-and-marketing cooperatives whenever and wherever this was feasible.[56] Since the state purchasing prices for agricultural goods were well below free market prices, the production teams as well as individual peasants tended to neglect the production for the state in favor of producing for the market. These conflicting interests placed the local cadres in a position of receiving pressures from above and a demand from below that made them very vulnerable to corruption.

The Party leaders were alarmed that the private-sector activities in the rural areas had become too widespread and might possibly grow out of control. In March 1963, the leadership launched a new "anti-five evils" campaign, namely against "corruption and embezzlement, speculation, extravagance and waste, decentralism, and bureaucracy" in the governmental organs and enterprises at and above the county level. In the middle of the same year, the Party started a "Socialist Education Movement" in the rural areas, aiming to execute what was termed the "four cleanups," constituting efforts to clean things up in the fields of politics, ideology, organization, and the economy.[57] The government sent thousands of its staff to rural areas to mobilize the masses to expose the "evils of capitalist thinking and customs" of rural cadres such as corruption, embezzlement, and other violations of the law and the party's discipline. The purge intensified after the Central Committee of the Party estimated in the summer of 1964 that "the leadership in about one-third of the rural grass-roots organizations was not in the hands of the people."[58] By 1965, governmental organs at all levels reportedly had sent between one-third and one-half of their personnel to investigate abuses of socialist morality in rural areas by "eating, living, working, and discussing together with poor and lower-middle peasants."[59]

The hardline policy toward the rural private economy was most severe in the early years of the Cultural Revolution (1966 to 1969) as the Maoist leaders gained control of the Party's administration organs. They resumed some abandoned practices of the people's commune in rural areas.[60] The radical leaders attacked the liberalization policies of the early 1960s as schemes to restore capitalism in China. Attacks were concentrated on the policy of Liu Shao-qi's "three freedoms and one contract."[61] The idiom referred to private plots, free markets, and household sideline occupations, as the three freedoms, and to the fixed contract that specified each household's compulsory sale of agricultural goods to the state. In many areas, while the commune system underwent radical changes in organization, private plots were once again confiscated and sideline occupations and rural fairs were banned since they represented a "survival of capitalism." In 1968, there were even provisions prohibiting the members of rural people's communes from engaging in all commercial activities.[62]

These radical policies were responsible for the stagnation in agricultural production in the early years of the Cultural Revolution. Facing the troubles in agriculture, the Party was forced again to switch back to pragmatic alternatives. In 1970, Premier Zhou En-lai chaired a State Council conference on agricultural issues. In this conference, the government reinitiated most of the pragmatic policies concerning the people's commune, including policies that legitimized private plots, household sideline production, and rural fairs.[63] Free rural markets were tolerated, at least regionally, and sometimes even officially condoned as a means of activating the rural economy. However, the implementation of these relatively liberal policies was never smooth in the Cultural Revolution because of the dominant influence of Maoist ideology. For instance, in 1970, a government directive stipulated that except state-run commercial establishments, marketing-and-supply cooperatives, and a small number of licensed peddlers, no other units or individuals were allowed to engage in trading. By September of 1971, half of the production brigades and teams in the Jiangxi Province had been financially merged to communes, and two-thirds of private plots were taken away by the communes.[64] In 1975, Mao raised the issue that "bourgeois rights" in the form of the existing wage and commodity system "should be restricted under the dictatorship of the proletariat." Following this instruction, the Party became concerned with the "small production that engenders capitalism and the bourgeoisie" in the rural economy.[65] The previously tolerated rural fair practice came under attack again. Consequently, total subordination of rural trading to the appropriate Party command was categorically demanded in the name of "building socialist rural fairs." The official press also announced in 1975 that all marketing-and-supply cooperatives were to be merged with state-run commercial establishments, all urban fairs were to be closed down, and rural fairs were to be strictly limited.[66]

The radical policy toward the rural private economy continued for the first two years following Mao's death in 1976. Hua Guofeng, Mao's chosen successor and the chairman of the Party then, initiated a nationwide campaign to learn from Mao's model production brigade, Dazhai. The model, a village in Northwestern China, had been well known for its nonmaterial incentives in association with communist morality, semi-military discipline, egalitarian income distribution, frugality of the lives of its members, and reliance upon revolutionary fervor to achieve progress in productivity. Hua vowed to transform one third of the counties into the Dazhai-type by 1980.[67] In the campaign of "learning from Dazhai," rural private plots, household sideline production, and trading fairs were either restricted or discouraged because of their so-called "capitalist tendencies."[68]

5.5 Street Peddlers under Suppression

The fate of urban handicraftsmen and peddlers was similar to that of their rural counterparts. Although the urban private sector in the Mao era had been negligibly small, the official attitude toward it was a touchstone of the general economic policy. Whenever the Maoist leaders gained dominant control of the Party's administration organs, the private sector was either completely banned or deliberately restricted. Whenever the national economy was in great difficulty and the supply of necessities for the populace was threatened, the leadership would be forced to adopt a relatively pragmatic attitude toward the private sector. Generally, however, under Mao's reign, the urban private sector was squeezed to the brink of extinction.

By the end of the Socialist Transformation period (1956) private handicraftsmen and peddlers almost ceased to exist. The number of people engaged in private businesses declined sharply from 1953 to 1956. In 1957, under the leadership of Chen Yun, private business in handicraft and small retail commerce was again on the rise. However, in 1958, the year of the Great Leap Forward, many handicraft cooperatives organized in the period of the Socialist Transformation were ordered to be reorganized into state-owned factories. In this year, 36 percent of the handicraft cooperatives were transformed to state ownership and 35 percent were incorporated into the new rural communes.[69]

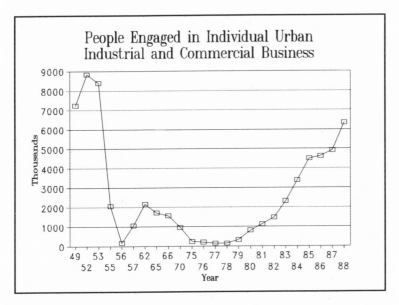

Figure 5.2
Source: *Almanac of China's Economy* 1984-1990; *China Social Statistics 1986.*

During the liberalization that followed the disastrous Great Leap Forward, the government stipulated that handicraft cooperatives or groups that had been transformed into state-owned or commune-owned industrial enterprises during the Great Leap Forward period (1958 to 1960) should be resolutely switched back. In 1961, the Party drew up "Some Regulations for Improving Commercial Work," which stated that supply-and-marketing cooperatives and rural fairs were as important as state-owned commercial enterprises as channels for commodity circulation, and therefore should be restored and retained.[70] In 1962, the year of economic retrenchment, in order to overcome the state budget difficulties, the government closed down all the commune-operated enterprises and returned many of them to handicraft cooperatives and even as family sideline occupations.[71] To help unemployed workers survive by engaging in self-employed businesses, the government issued more peddler licenses. As a result, the number of people engaging in individual industrial and commercial business greatly increased in the early 1960s. During the Cultural Revolution, however, the private sector shrank again. In the name of "cutting the tails of capitalism," private handicraftsmen and peddlers were under heavy bombardment from radical attacks, and were almost eliminated in the urban area. Figure 5.2 shows the sharp decline of the number of people in the private sector during the Socialist Transformation and the private sector's temporary recovery in the early 1960s.[72]

5.6 The Business Lurking Underground

During the Mao era, while private businesses were openly suppressed in both rural and urban areas, an underground private economy grew quietly. The most prominent was the black market trade of coupons and rationed goods that prevailed in urban areas. After the state compulsory procurement of major agricultural goods was established in the first half of the 1950s, a nationwide rationing system was introduced.[73] Food rationing began with grain and edible oils, and soon spread to a wide range of subsidiary foodstuffs such as sugar, pork, and bean-made food. A number of non-food consumer goods, mainly daily necessities and durables in shortage, also became rationed through the years.[74] The food rationing system had several characteristics: First, it was implemented through the household registration system, and strictly excluded rural residents. Second, city dwellers were classified into different categories, for the purpose of rationing, according to their residential region, age, career, and political rank. Third, different cities had quite different lists of rationed goods and rationed quotas. Finally, the number and categories of rationing coupons fluctuated through years depending on general and local economic situations. For instance, in the most difficult years after the disastrous Great Leap Forward, meat was rationed 0.1 kilograms per month per urban resident; cotton cloth 2 meter per year per urban resident.[75] These characteristics inspired speculative trade of rationing coupons and rationed goods among people of different social rankings and from different regions, especially between urban residents and peasants. Ration coupons usually played the role of quasi money in the black market. Individual peasants and also the communes and production brigades purchased agricultural goods at rural fairs for shipment to urban black markets. Urban residents, cooperatives, and even state enterprises, government offices, and army units illicitly purchased these agricultural goods.[76]

Apart from the prevalence of the black market, the workmanship of state employees degenerated significantly. The early zeal that had characterized mass mobilization ebbed through the years of political struggle. By restraining wage increase, the government curbed the purchasing power of consumers to enforce price stability in an economy of shortage. Between 1963 and 1977, while the general price level remained almost unchanged, the wages for most workers were virtually frozen except for some minor adjustments.[77] During the Cultural Revolution, the radical leaders abolished the bonus system in state enterprises.[78] The real wage declined continuously. The annual growth rate of average real wage was -1.2 percent for the period 1966 to 1970 and -0.1 percent for the period 1971 to 1975.[79] The persistence of low wages and an egalitarian distribution severely affected the motivation of workers.

Besides that, the management of state-run enterprises was tremendously weakened in the Great Leap Forward and the Cultural Revolution. The management ideals of the Maoists were reducing staff, ranks, and rules.[80] Under these ideals, the professional management divisions and offices had been abolished repeatedly, and rules and regulations had been scrapped. For instance, the management system of one-man responsibility, which was a key part of the vertical command structure introduced from the Soviet Union in the early 1950s, was abolished in 1956. The main reason behind this was that the system seemed to conflict with the authority of the Party committee at the enterprise level and Mao's principles that the Party should always command economic work.[81] In the retrenchment period following the Great Leap Forward, the authority of enterprise managers was reaffirmed.[82] However, during the Cultural Revolution, the radicals charged this management system with suppressing initiative of workers, and purged a great number of executives. In addition, mass mobilization for political reasons brought chaos to enterprise management. In 1967, the labor discipline in enterprises was so relaxed that the rate of attendance in the nation's coal mines was only about fifty to sixty percent, and the utility rate of work was only four to five hours a day.[83] Many managerial rules were abandoned or frequently violated during the Cultural Revolution. In many enterprises, production could hardly proceed normally, the quality of products declined, the number of accidents increased, and productivity stagnated.[84] Because of this mess in management, production efficiency of the state-owned enterprises deteriorated drastically (Table 5.1).

Table 5.1   Efficiency Indicators of the State-Owned Enterprises

Year	Taxes and Profits Generated Per 100 Yuan Fund	Taxes and Profits Generated Per 100 Yuan Fixed Assets	Profits Per 100 Yuan Gross Industrial Product Value
1966	35.7	46.7	24.9
1976	20.1	28.8	11.8

Source: *Almanac of China's Economy 1989*, II: p. 21.

In addition to the deterioration of management, continuous political turmoil also deprived Chinese society of a stable framework of law and order. For many people there was no longer legal constraint on their personal interest seeking. The only thing they would be concerned with was the feasibility of a specific action. This norm of social cynicism inevitably resulted in rampant illegal rent-seeking activities in the Chinese economy, where state employees had been denied legitimate material incentives for years, and where plenty of contrived surpluses and rents existed due to the shortage of goods, distorted prices, and slack management of state property. Therefore, in the Mao era, the "backdoor deals" that involved illegitimate monetary or non-monetary exchange of favors, as de facto bribes in the forms of goods or services in shortage, grew to an important social phenomenon. This usually involved pilfering and bribery among employees of state-run enterprises. This practice was so common that it became an open secret since management in state-owned enterprises was slack and the poorly paid workers felt that this activity was fair compensation for their low and frozen pay.[85]

5.7 Concluding Comments

The experience of the private sector during the Mao era supports the theoretical results located in the earlier part of this book. First, the entrepreneurial activities, in the form of non-planned production and trade, rural and urban private businesses, and the underground economy activities, appeared to be highly sensitive to the changes in institutions and the wavering of official economic policies.

Second, it seems that the Chinese society never experienced a complete lack of entrepreneurship under the communist regime, even in the most suppressive years of the Mao era. After the Socialist Transformation, although the Maoist leaders attempted to eradicate the remnant private sector through repeated political campaigns and ruthless economic crackdowns, private entrepreneurs exhibited a tenacious ability to survive in the rifts of the planned economy. Following every wave of political persecution and economic crackdown, private entrepreneurial activity always revived miraculously. Besides the open private sector in rural and urban areas, the underground economic activities in the form of black market trade and "backdoor deals" were prevalent among urban residents and employees of state-owned enterprises.

The major problem of entrepreneurial activities in this period can be interpreted in terms of entrepreneurial resource allocation. As the government imposed stern restrictions on private entrepreneurship in the production of goods and services, much of society's entrepreneurial resource was forced to fuel the underground backdoor deal trading or bribe-exchange. When people engaged in this type of activity, they sought the contrived surpluses in the goods and services in shortage. Although gains generally exceeded costs for individuals, the costs of the underground trade contained little productive expense and the activity hardly increased the real supply of goods and services in shortage. The improvement of the individuals' economic welfare in the underground trade could have been achieved at a much lower transaction cost in a free market economy. Meanwhile, the development of this type of activity in the Mao era appeared to be a passive individual reaction to the institutional constraints and did not have enough momentum to cause institutional innovations favoring productive entrepreneurial activity. The role of the underground trade was therefore similar to that of the "non-suppliers' surplus-seeking" described in Chapter 3, which leads to the generation of wastes for society and does not help society correct the distortions in the economy.

Moreover, the relative payoffs of entrepreneurial activities in the Mao era highly favored those unproductive activities in the form of political speculation for personal gains, bribery, and pilfering. On the one hand, we find that the denial of material incentives discouraged the entrepreneurship necessary for the better management of production. Productive entrepreneurship, even in the state sector, was repeatedly depressed for political reasons. While on the other hand, the destruction of a stable legal framework and economic order of China's centrally planned economy increased the effectiveness of horizontal rent-seeking through pilfering and bribery. Consequently, entrepreneurial talents were widely misused and the Chinese economy in the Mao era suffered great losses in productivity.

NOTES

1. Many studies have been done on the issue of the power struggle between the two factions in the Chinese Communist Party. Some of these are: Harding, Harry, *China's Second Revolution: Reform after Mao*, Washington, D.C.: The Brookings Institution, 1987, pp. 11-20; Chang, David Wen-wei, *China Under Deng Xiaoping*, New York: St. Martin's Press, 1988, pp. 21-44; Cheng, C. op. cit., pp. 29-55; Lardy, Nicholas R. and Kenneth Lieberthal ed., *Chen Yun's Strategy for China's Development—— a Non-Maoist Alternative*, New York: M.E. Sharpe, Inc., 1983, "Introduction"; and Whitson, W., "The Political Dynamics of the P.R.C.," Joint Economic Committee, *Chinese Economy Post Mao: a Compendium of Papers*, Washington, D.C.: Joint Committee Print, 1978, pp. 63-79.

2. When the de-Maoization from 1978 to 1980 reached its height, the Party leadership restrained itself to further demotion of Mao's thoughts because it realized that no other systematic thought could replace Mao's thoughts by that time if the Party was to remain in power. The Communist Party's 1981 Resolution on Questions of the Party History held that Mao's thoughts were "the valuable spiritual asset of our Party. It will be our guide to action for a long time to come." [Quoted from Liu and Wu ed., op. cit., appendix, p. 578.]

3. This was reflected by Mao's "basic line of socialist historical stage." See the offical journal of the Communist Party of China (CPC), *Hongqi* (Red Flag), Beijing, China: No.10, 1967, for a description.

4. Liu Shao-qi was the chairman of the People's Republic in the period from 1959 to 1968. He was the main target of the Cultural Revolution (1966-76) and died in 1969.

5. Liu Shao-qi, *Political Report of the Central Committee of the CPC to the Eighth National Congress*, Beijing, China: Foreign Language Press, 1956, pp. 15-6.

6. Mao Zedong, *Selected Works of Mao Zedong* (5 vols.), Beijing, China: Foreign Language Press, 1965-77, vol. 5, pp. 218-24.

7. Snow, Edgar, *Red China Today*, Harmondsworth: Penguin Books, 1970, p. 421.

8. Liu and Wu ed., op. cit., p. 233.

9. *Hongqi* (Red Flag), No. 16 (16 August 1960), p. 3.

10. Cheng, op. cit., p. 37.

11. Ch'en, Jerome ed., *Mao Papers: Anthology and Bibliography*, Cambridge: Oxford University Press, 1970, pp. 103-05.

12. Quoted from Bouc, Alain, *Mao Tse-tung: A Guide to His Thought*, New York: St. Martin's Press, 1977, p. 143.

13. Liu Guoguan and Wang Ruisun, "Restructuring of the Economy," in *China's Socialist Modernization*, Yu Guangyuan ed., Beijing: Foreign Language Press, 1984, pp. 90-94.

14. Lardy and Lieberthal ed., op. cit. pp. 18-22.

15. Mao believed that "of all the things in the world, people are the most precious. As long as there are people, every kind of miracle can be performed under the leadership of the Communist Party." [Mao, op. cit., vol. 4, p. 454.]

16. *Renmin Ribao* (People's Daily), 29 December 29 1968, p. 1.

17. In 1975, a year before his death, Mao issued a comment on the socialist principle of "to each according to one's work" and the existing wage and commodity system. He strongly indicated that these were "bourgeois rights" and "should be restricted under the dictatorship of the proletariat." Mao also expressed his disgust of any trail of private economic activity by mentioning Lenin's thesis that "small production engenders capitalism and the bourgeoisie continuously daily, hourly, spontaneously, and on a mass scale." [Liu and Wu ed., op. cit., p. 400.]

18. Cheng, op. cit., p. 214.

19. One of Mao's well-known ideas was: "humble people are the most intelligent, and high ranking figures the most stupid." [Bouc, op. cit., p. 200.]

20. Lardy and Lieberthal ed., op. cit., pp. 21-22.

21. Wu, Yuan-li. *The Economy of Communist China*, New York: Praeger, 1965, p. 28.

22. See Cheng, op. cit., Chapter 6 for a more detailed account.

23. Cheng, op. cit., pp. 171-172.

24. The worst year of the Cultural Revolution, 1968, was the only year without a national economic annual plan since central planning was introduced into China. [Liu and Wu, op. cit., p. 349.]

25. *Hongqi* (Red Flag), No. 11, 1 June 1980, pp. 2-5.

26. Donnithorne, Audrey, *China's Economic System*, London: Allen and Unwin, 1967, p. 459; Kraus, op. cit., pp. 71-2.

27. Lardy, N., "Economic Planning in the People's Republic of China: Central-Provincial Fiscal Relations," U.S. Congress, Joint Economic Committee, *China: A Reassessment of the Economy*, Washington, D.C.: Joint Committee Print, 1975, p. 99.

28. Kraus, op. cit., pp. 79-80.

29. Prybyla, Jan S., *The Political Economy of Communist China*, Scranton, Pennsylvania: International Textbook Company, 1970, pp. 234-235.

30. See the Eighth Central Committee of the CPC, "Resolution on Some Questions Concerning the People's Communes," *Xinhua Banyuekan* (New China Biweekly), Beijing, China, No. 24, December 1958, pp. 7-8.

31. Kraus, op. cit., p. 141.

32. See Liu and Wu, op. cit., p. 277 for a more detailed discussion.

33. Kraus, op. cit., p. 141.

34. Liu and Wu, op. cit., p. 364

35. Liu and Wu, op. cit., pp. 379-381.

36. Prybyla, op. cit., p. 275.

37. Liu and Wu, op. cit., pp. 353-54.

38. Liu and Wu, op. cit., p. 368.

39. Xue Muqiao, *Zhongguo Shehuizhuyi Jingji Wenti Yanjiu* (Study of China's Socialist Economic Problems), Beijing: People's Press, 1979, pp. 108-109.

40. Ibid, pp. 368-69.

41. Yan Shikuai, "Strive to Complete 'Unfinished Construction Projects'," *Renmin Ribao* (People's Daily), 25 September, 1978, p. 3.

42. Donnithorne, Audrey, "China's Cellular Economy: Some Economic Trends since the Cultural Revolution," *China Quarterly*, Vol. 52, 1972, pp. 605-612.

43. Liu and Wu, op. cit., p. 362.

44. Wu Xiang, "On the Development of Township and Village Industries," Almanac Editorial Board ed., *Zhongguo Jingji Nianjian* (Almanac of China's Economy) [*Almanac of China's Economy* hereafter], Beijing: Publisher of Beijing Journal of Economic Management, 1986, Vol. II, pp. 15-18.

45. Xue Muqiao, "The Evolution of the Ownership of Production Means in China," *Jingji Yanjiu* (Economic Research) [Beijing, China], No. 2, 1982, pp. 18-19.

46. Ibid., p. 45.

47. In Chinese agriculture, the government assigns government purchasing quota volumes to farmers or their collectives. The list prices for these quota volumes are much lower than free market prices. Also, when the government wishes to purchase additional farm and sideline products, it may pay the above-quota markup prices, which are a certain percentage higher than the list prices, but usually lower than free market prices. The percentage markup is set by the government. Sometimes, the government pays the "negotiated prices," which are roughly equal to free market prices. The state purchasing prices are the weighted average of these three prices paid by the government. *China Trade and Price Statistics 1988*, New York: Praeger Publishers, 1989, p. xv.

48. Lardy and Lieberthal ed., op. cit., pp. 21-22.

49. Prybyla, op. cit., pp. 233-234.

50. Cheng, op. cit., p. 103.

51. For the research on the consequences of famine in the period, see Chen Qiming, "Estimations on Population Change During the Great Leap Forward," *Zhongguo Zhi Chun* (China Spring) [Flushing, New York], No.11 1988 (66), pp. 63-66.

52. Prybyla, op. cit., p. 287, p. 298.

53. Donnithorne, 1967, p. 298.

54. Prybyla, op. cit., pp. 350-351.

55. See Liu and Wu ed. op. cit., pp. 310-311, and Kraus, op. cit., p. 153.

56. Liu and Wu ed., op. cit., p. 310.

57. Ibid., p. 301, p. 308.

58. Ibid., p. 310.

59. Prybyla, op. cit., pp. 358-59.

60. Cheng, op. cit., pp. 109-110.

61. Kraus, op. cit., p. 182.

62. Liu and Wu ed., op. cit., p. 410.

63. Ibid., p. 376, pp. 381-82.

64. Ibid., p. 381, p. 410.

65. Ibid., pp. 400-01.

66. Ibid., pp. 410-11.

67. Hua Guofeng, "Speech at the Second National Conference on Learning From Dazhai in Agriculture," *Beijing Review*, Vol. 20, no. 1, 1 Jan. 1977, pp. 31-44.

68. *Zhongguo Jingji Nianjian* (Almanac of China's Economy) 1989, II: p. 21; Liu and Wu ed., op. cit., pp. 430-1.

69. Xue Muqiao, Su Xing, and Lin Zili, op. cit., p. 157.

70. Donnithorne, 1967, pp. 231-32.

71. Ibid., pp. 230-31.

72. Another estimate shows that the number of people engaging in individual industrial and commercial business was only 430 thousand in 1961, but jumped to three million by the end of 1962. [Xu Bangtai, "The Rise and Fall of Individual Economy and Its Impacts on Current Mainland China's Society," *Zhongguo Zhi Chun* (China Spring), No.11 1988 (66), pp. 19-24]

73. The State Council of the PRC, "Provisional Measures for Handling Urban Fixed Grain Supply," *Xinhua Yuebao* (New China Monthly) [Beijing, China], No.9, 28 Sept. 1955, pp. 163-4.

74. For a more detailed account, see Perkins, Dwight, *Market Control and Planning in Communist China*, Cambridge: Harvard University

Press, 1966, and Cheng, op. cit., pp. 204-209.

75. *Zhongguo Jingji Nianjian* (Almanac of China's Economy) 1989, p. II-19.

76. This has been "an open secret" in China for years. For example, see Liaoning Provincial Revolutionary Committee "Circular Forbids Unauthorized Purchase of Goods," *Foreign Broadcasting Information Service*, 18 October 1978, pp. L6-L7.

77. Cheng, op. cit., p. 248.

78. See Yao Wenyuan, "On the Social Basis of the Lin Biao Anti-Party Clique," *Hongqi* (Red Flag), No.3 (March) 1975.

79. *Zhongguo Tongji Nianjian* (Statistical Yearbook of China) 1991, p. 130.

80. White, Lynn T. *Policies of Chaos: The Organizational Causes of Violence in China's Cultural Revolution*, Princeton, New Jersey: Princeton University Press, p. 263.

81. The Communist Party of China (CPC), *The Eighth National Congress of the CPC*, Beijing: Foreign Language Press, 1957, Vol. 11, pp. 304-306.

82. Donnithorne, 1967, p. 198.

83. Liu and Wu ed., op. cit., p. 354.

84. Ibid., p. 421.

85. The word "back-door deals" was invented in the Cultural Revolution. Many people were impressed and surprised by the sudden prevalence of the practice during the first few years of the Cultural Revolution. For instance, in her factual account of what she experienced in the Cultural Revolution, Nien Cheng vividly describes the back-door network that had developed during that period [See Nien Cheng, *Life and Death in Shanghai*, New york: Grove Press, 1986]. For a more theoretical analysis, see Fung op. cit.

CHAPTER 6

THE PRIVATE PIONEERS OF REFORMS

6.1 Introduction

In December 1978, two years after Mao's death, the pragmatic elites led by Deng Xiaoping got the upper hand of the Party leadership in the Third Plenary of the Eleventh CPC Central Committee. This event was hailed as "a crucial turning point of far-reaching significance."[1] After the Plenary, the Chinese economy embarked on a comprehensive reform. The market-oriented reform in the 1980s brought drastic changes to China's economic structure and a successful economic taking-off to the country.

This chapter reviews some major reforms in the 1980s and evaluates the role of private entrepreneurs in those reforms. An important observation is that, in the reforms, the evolution of the institutional environment of the private economy was a result of the interaction between policy-makers' pragmatic consideration and private entrepreneurs' innovative activities. In the future, the similar interaction is likely to continue and further expansion of the non-state sectors can be expected.

Section 6.2 briefly pictures the overall revival of the private sector and the boom of other non-state sectors in the 1980s. Section 6.3 depicts the official guideline for reform as a mixture of pragmatic considerations and ideological constraints. It shows that, under the changing official guideline, the government policy toward the private sector was inherently ambiguous. Both Section 6.4 and Section 6.5 examine the adjustment of official policies toward non-state sectors in the 1980s. The data in these sections highlights the contribution of private entrepreneurs to reforms in the rural and urban areas. In the concluding section we will relate private entrepreneurs' role in China's reform to some theoretical results of the previous chapters. These results shed light on the potential social cost of the reform process reviewed in this chapter.

6.2 An Overall Revival of the Private Sector

The boom of the private and other non-state sectors drastically changed China's economic structure in the 1980s. During the decade the Chinese economy evolved into a mixed structure (Figure 6.1 and Figure 6.2). The real ownership structure may be more complicated than the conventional categorization suggests. Joint enterprises developed among state, collective, and private enterprises, and even foreign companies. Different kinds of ownership interweave with each other. Even within the state-owned sector there were experiments in ownership reform in the late 1980s. These include: leasing small state-owned enterprises to collectives or even individuals, transforming the unique ownership of large state-owned enterprises through stock issuing, and so forth.[2]

The first driving force of this structural change was the revival of the household peasant economy. In pre-reform Chinese agriculture, peasants were organized into production teams (each of which included twenty to thirty households). The reward for their work was based upon the total revenue of the production team. From 1978 to 1983, the reforms in rural areas dismantled collective farming and revived traditional household farming.[3] Peasant households, which then started to cultivate land on long term leases, became independent firms in the agricultural sector. On the basis of this independence, peasants gradually attained further freedoms in their socioeconomic life during the 1980s. These included the freedom to re-contract tenant land to other farmers, the freedom to own and run non-agricultural business, and the freedom to run commercial business beyond the local area.[4] These changes provided opportunities for peasants to run private or collective business in industry and commerce.

Figure 6.1 Shares of Gross Output Value
of Industry by Ownership 1980-1990
(In Percentage of Total Output Value)

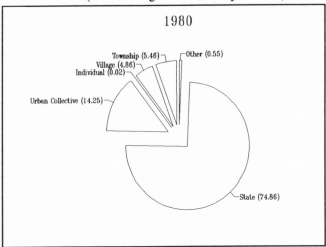

Figure 6.1 (a)

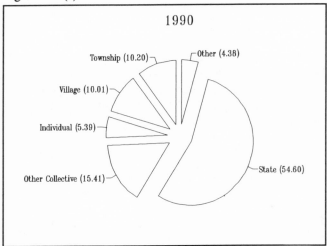

Figure 6.1 (b)

Source: *China Statistical Abstracts; Statistical Yearbook of China.*

Note: The "other" category includes joint state-collective, joint state-private, and joint collective-private enterprises, foreign-Chinese joint ventures, enterprises run by overseas Chinese, businessmen from Hong Kong and Macao, and enterprises run by foreigners. The "other collective" category in 1990 includes urban collective enterprises, urban and rural joint collective enterprises and all other forms of collective enterprises.

Figure 6.2 Shares of Retail Sales
by Ownership of Selling Agents (1977-1990)
(In Percentage of Total Sale Value)

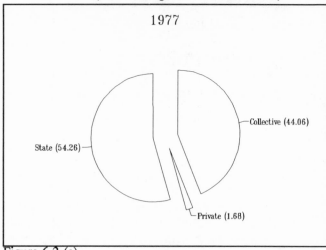

Figure 6.2 (a)

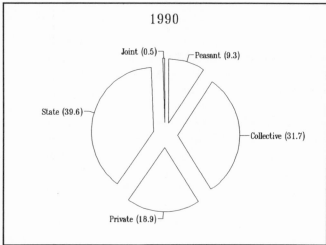

Figure 6.2 (b)

Source: *China Trade and Price Statistics* 1988; *Almanac of China's Commerce* 1991.

Note: The "private" category includes individual merchants and retail sales by agricultural to non-agricultural residents. The "peasant" category refers to sales by peasants to urban residents.

Before the economic reform, years of political campaigns against "capitalist tendencies" almost eliminated private businesses in China. After 1978 the "individual business" rapidly revived (see the note in Table 6.1 for the definition of "individual business.") Table 6.1 shows a summary of these changes.

Table 6.1   The Number of People Engaged in "Individual" Industrial and Commercial Business (Thousands)

(The numbers in brackets are the number of enterprises)

Year	1953	1956	1965	1978	1980	1981	1983	1988	1989
Urban	8380	160	1710	140	801	1030	2310 (1706)	6330 (3383)	6480 (3400)
Total						2249	7465 (5901)	23049 (14527)	19320 (12430)

Source: *Almanac of China's Economy* (1984), (1988); *Renmin Ribao (People's Daily)*'s related reports; *China Rural Statistics* (1988); *Statistical Yearbook of China* (1991).
Note:
a. China's official statistic document defines those private business firms employing fewer than 8 people as "individual business"; otherwise "private enterprises." [Almanac of China's Economy (1988), p. XI:157.]
b. No statistics of rural individual business were officially collected before 1981.

The growth of "individual business" was unprecedented in the history of the People's Republic of China. As shown in Table 6.1, the total number of people engaged in business in 1988 was ten times as many as in 1981. This represented an increase at 39.44 percent annually from 1981 to 1988. For the period before the 1980s, the number of people engaged in rural private business was negligible and seldom mentioned in official statistics. It was not until 1983 that peasants were officially allowed to run individual business in non-agricultural sectors.[5]

The reform in rural areas created the climate for private non-agricultural business to grow in the early 1980s and the latter became the major force of private business. Up to 1986, the growth of "individual business" in rural areas was faster than that in urban areas. As a result, during 1981 to 1987, the percentage of private business people engaged in urban "individual business" declined from 45.8 percent to 22.81 percent. In the late 1980s, the growth rate of urban "individual business" began to surpass that of rural business, but rural private firms continued to be the main force in "individual business."[6]

The size of private businesses also increased in the 1980s. In the early 1980s, the average number of people engaged per "individual business" was 1.2.[7] In 1989, the number rose to 1.55 (computed from Table 6.1). A more significant phenomenon was the rise of "private enterprises" after the mid-1980s.[8] Most of the "private enterprises" developed upon the base of "individual businesses" and more than 80 percent were located in rural areas.[9] In 1987 about 30 percent of the enterprises were firms with more than 20 employees and one percent of the enterprises had more than 100 employees. Because a number of private enterprises registered themselves as "collective enterprises" and "joint enterprises" for tax benefits, the real number of private enterprises usually exceeds the number of the registered ones. An official estimate put the number of private enterprises in 1987 as 225 thousand, employing 3.6 million people, 0.68 percent of the nation's total labor force.[10] An unofficial investigation in 1988, however, estimated that people engaged in the private economy nationwide (including "individual businesses" and "private enterprises") had exceeded 30 million, accounting 5.52 percent of national labor force.[11]

A phenomenal aspect of the growth of the non-state sectors was the boom of township and village enterprises. The first upsurge of these enterprises, formerly called "commune and brigade enterprises," occurred in the early 1970s, when the central government took measures to implement Mao's thesis of "walking on two legs."[12] Before the 1980s, however, in most areas the growth of rural local small industries had been slow. These industries, generally excluded from the state plans, had little chance to develop.

In the early 1980s, as household farming revived in rural areas, the rural township and village enterprises began to boom at an unprecedented pace. The boom accelerated after 1984, the year in which the central government adopted a positive attitude toward these industries.[13] The average annual increase of gross product value of these enterprises was 5.5 billion yuan for the period 1971 to 1978. Then it increased to 14.5 billion yuan for the period 1979 to 1983, and jumped to 99.65 billion yuan for the period 1984 to 1987.[14] Technology was greatly enhanced as these enterprises grew. During the period 1978 to 1988, the average size of township and village enterprises increased from 18.7 employees to 30.78 employees.[15] About 85 percent of the products met state standards of production. The total foreign exchange earnings of these enterprises exceeded US$10 billion in 1989, accounting for one fifth of the total export value.[16]

The importance of rural industries to the national economy multiplied during the 1980s. In 1978, only approximately five to six percent of the total national output value was produced by rural enterprises, but by 1989, this proportion had increased to about 25 percent.[17] In 1987, these enterprises employed 87.76 million people, compared with 99.84 million state employees in that year.[18] For the period 1986 to 1990, these enterprises accounted for 37.7 percent of the increase of national industrial product value. They also accounted for 28 percent of the increase of national foreign exchange earnings through export and 57.6 percent of new job opportunities.[19] In Jiangsu Province, the role of the township and village enterprises was more remarkable. In 1989 they accounted for more than half of the province's industrial output value, one fourth of the provincial government's revenue, and employed almost 30 percent of the rural labor force.[20]

The last but not the least driving force that changed China's economic structure in the 1980s was foreigners' direct investment. In the Mao era very few foreign companies were able to invest in China due to the official policy of "self-sufficiency." The open-door policies in the 1980s achieved significant results. From 1979 to 1989, more than 21,000 foreign-capital enterprises opened their business in China. The total used value of foreign direct investment was about $ 15.4 billion. Among these enterprises, more than seven percent were totally owned and run by foreigners, the rest were joint ventures.[21] Foreign-capital firms played a vital role in China's connection with the world economy. In 1989, one tenth of China's hard currency earnings through export came from the business of foreign-capital enterprises.[22]

6.3 Groping for Planted Stones

China's economic reform has effectively transferred the country toward a market economy. When the Party leadership started the process in the late 1970s, however, it did not conscientiously design the guideline for economic reform as market-oriented. After years of political turmoil of the Cultural Revolution, the Chinese leaders faced a severe economic reality. As a number of official documents in the late 1970s admitted, the Cultural Revolution had left Chinese economy at the verge of collapse. The most urgent task facing the Party and the government was to recover and develop the economy.[23] Therefore the senior leader Deng Xiaoping's pragmatism became the dominant principle of the Party's economic policy making. This pragmatism was expressed in Deng's well-known "cat thesis": "It does not matter whether cats are white or black; so long as they can catch mice, they are good cats."[24] A nationwide heated discussion of the "criterion of truth" in 1979 justified Deng's pragmatic thesis as a working principle of the Party: "Practice is the only test of truth."[25] This principle became a major vehicle for many of the reform schemes in the 1980s.

Deng's pragmatic thesis, however, remained officially within the framework of the Party's "four cardinal principles." These principles are: the socialist road (public ownership and central planning), the "people's democratic dictatorship," the sole leadership of the Communist Party, and the ideology of Marxism, Leninism, and Mao Zedong Thought. Therefore it has never been on the Party's agenda of reform to transfer the Chinese economy into a market economy in which private businesses play a dominant role. In the 1980s the so-called "moderate reformers," represented by Chen Yun, another senior leader, had important influence on the Party's economic policy making.[26] Chen and other moderate reformers consistently emphasized balanced growth under careful central planning. Their support for the introduction of market forces in the economy never went beyond the point that market plays a limited, supplementary role to central planning. In 1982, Chen proposed an analogy for his guideline of economic reform: The economy is like a bird, and the plan a cage; if the cage is too small, the bird will die; but if there is no cage at all, the bird will fly away, unconstrained.[27] The so-called "bird cage thesis" of Chen overshadowed the Party's blueprints of reform in the 1980s.

A major decision on the Third Plenary of the Party's Eleventh Central Committee (December 1978) was to switch the Party's focus from ideological work to economic development. On this plenary, however, the leadership did not propose specific long term goals for economic reform, except some rough ideas of decentralization and liberalization. The "Communique of the Third Plenary Session of the 11th Central Committee of the CPC" mentioned "the serious shortcomings in the structure of economic management" and "over-centralization of authority." The document suggested the necessity to decentralize decision-making powers, and the importance of the "law of value," which referred to market demand and supply.[28] With these vague ideas, first in agriculture, then in urban industry, the government launched a series of preliminary reforms designed to loosen control and provide better incentives. When some of these early reforms created serious imbalances in the economy, a central work conference at the end of 1980 adopted Chen Yun's proposal for retrenchment and readjustment.[29] In June 1981, the Party's Central Committee passed "The Resolution on Certain Questions in the History of the Party Since the Founding of the People's Republic of China (PRC)." The document stated a very limited scope for economic reform: "the state economy and the collective economy are the basic forms of the Chinese economy. The working people's individual economy within certain prescribed limits is a necessary complement to the public economy ... It is necessary to have a planned economy and at the same time give play to the supplementary, coordinating role of the market on the basis of public ownership. We must strive to promote commodity production and exchange on a socialist basis."[30]

On the Twelfth National Congress of the Communist Party of China (CPC) in September 1982, the then General Secretary Hu Yaobang presented in his political report a new guideline for reform. It compromised Chen Yun's economic thought with the need for further reforms.[31] According to Hu, the post-reform economy would include three major parts. Guiding plans would direct most economic activities through "economic levers" such as taxation, centrally-determined interest rates and prices. Mandatory planning would coordinate organization of large construction projects and the production and trade of some important products. The rest of the economy, those "unimportant" activities, should be totally left to free market coordination. Hu specified that reform would narrow the scope of mandatory planning and increase the scope of guiding planning. Under this guideline, the reformers managed to work out a series of economic reforms, the most important one being the legalization of the dual pricing system (two-track price system) in material supply.[32]

In October 1984, the Central Committee of the CPC's "Decision on Reform of the Economic Structure" modified the official guideline by proposing to build a "planned commodity economy." The document gave the first official statement that the nature of the post-reform economy should be a "planned commodity economy" (i.e., a planned market economy) and "law of value" [market demand and supply] must be consciously followed and applied. A planned economy "does not necessarily mean the predominance of mandatory planning." Again, the "Decision" maintained that this "planned commodity economy" should be based on public ownership. "Production and exchange completely subject to market coordination are confined mainly to certain farm and sideline products, small articles of daily use and labor services in the service and repair traders." All of these will "play a supplementary but indispensable role in the national economy." The "Decision" asserted that China's "individual economy" was different from capitalist private economy for being part of the "socialist economy." It also suggested that the "individual economy" should be encouraged especially in "those economic activities mainly involving labor service and appropriate for decentralized operation." [33]

The official guideline for reform reached its most "radical" form on the Thirteenth National Congress of the CPC in October 1987. The then General Secretary Zhao Ziyang, in his political report, proposed a new thesis of a post-reform economy that resembles a regulated market economy: "the state adjusts the market, the market guides enterprises." In this "new economic mechanism," the state will "use economic, legislative, and necessary administrative means to adjust market demand and supply, creating proper economic and social environment, through which to guide enterprises to make management decisions properly." [34] He also denied the merit of mandatory planning by announcing that mandatory planning "cannot meet the requirement of developing the socialist commodity economy." According to him, the structure of "socialist planned commodity economy" should be the one that unifies plan and market in itself. [35] Zhao also broke the restrictions on the scope of market exchange defined in the 1984 "Decision on Reform." Instead he advocated the development of factor markets of capital, labor, technology, and real estate. [36] Although he maintained that the main body of the ownership structure should be public, Zhao claimed that the non-state sectors had not developed too much but far from enough. Therefore he insisted on the continuance of the Party's policy to encourage the "individual" and "private" businesses. In the first two years after Zhao's dismissal during the 1989 Tiananmen Square Event, this guideline for reform was substantially revised in official documents. [37]

The evolution of the Party's guideline for reform in the 1980s reflects a carefully-kept balance between ideological doctrines and pragmatic consideration of economic reality. At the peak of economic reform in the late 1980s, the cornerstone of the reform was the so-called "theory of the primary period of socialism." The theory appeared in Zhao's report on the Thirteenth National Congress of the CPC. It views contemporary China as a "socialist society built on an economic base of low productivity and low living standards." Due to the backwardness of the economy, a very long "primary period of socialism" is necessary for China to accomplish "industrialization, commercialization, socialization, and modernization of production." Many other countries, however, have accomplished this process under the capitalist system.[38] The theory provided important ideological support provided for reform. According to the theory, the full development of "the commodity economy" (i.e., the market economy) is "a period that cannot be skipped in socioeconomic evolution." The market economy is "an indispensable basic condition for realizing the socialization and modernization of production."[39] Obviously, this theory was cautiously designed within the "four cardinal principles" as a revision to the traditional Marxist doctrines of social evolution.

The pragmatic adjustment of the official guideline and its carefully-kept balance with the Party's ideological principles characterized the step-by-step, piecemeal reforms in the 1980. At least until the "planned commodity economy" was proposed as the goal of reform in 1984, the decision makers did not purposely design the reform schemes to transfer the economy toward a market economy. Throughout the 1980s there were dividing ideas within the leadership about the nature of the post-reform "planned commodity economy." As vividly suggested by Deng that as reform is something new, the Party and the government "have to grope around to find our way like crossing the river while groping for stones planted at the bottom."[40] This "strategy" has left a relatively free exploration for reform but also reflects the lack of a consistent long-term approach to reform.

When the issue of private business was in concern, the official policies were usually ambiguous and confusing. On the one hand, the authorities allowed and even encouraged the development of the private sector to some extent in the 1980s. On the other hand, the Party never showed willingness to accept a general privatization policy during the decade. Instead the Party leaders repeatedly asserted that the post-reform economy should be based on public ownership. The development of the private economy "should never weaken or replace the dominant status of the public owned economy," not to mention leading to any privatization.[41] To a large extent, the Chinese policy makers did not pre-design the boom of the private sector in the 1980s and the relating changes in institutions. In many cases, what happened was the official adaption to reforms initiated by private entrepreneurs. The government sometimes played a role of "followership" rather than leadership in economic reform. The evolution of the legal framework and policy environment of the private economy in the 1980s was essentially a result of the interaction between official policy changes and private entrepreneurs' institutional innovation.

6.4 The Peasant-Reformers

The rural economic reform in the late 1970s and early 1980s was well known for its success in promoting agricultural productivity. A less well-known aspect of the reform was a series of government concessions to private entrepreneurs' spontaneous activities.

The major breakthrough of this reform happened in the early 1980s when the contract responsibility system (especially the contract-production-to-household practice) prevailed nationwide in rural areas. Under the contract-production-to-household practice, the collective authorities allocate each household a certain amount of land on a long-term basis with the household to receive all income from the land after meeting certain obligations to the collective and the state. This system divided the collectively-owned means of production, including tools and land, among individual households. It was therefore a de facto de-collectivization and restoration of household tenant farming. This measure, however, was not a new invention during the rural reform in the 1980s. It emerged in some areas as a remedy for the bankrupt rural economy during the post-Great Leap Forward retrenchment in the early 1960s.[42] In the Mao era the experiment of contract-production-to-household was short-lived: it was soon abandoned and severely attacked as a "capitalist crime." Thousands of peasants and rural cadres were persecuted for their de-collectivization deeds.[43]

The post-Mao rural reform originated in Anhui Province in 1978, which was experiencing a ten-month long drought.[44] A severe famine threatened thousands of peasants' lives. In desperation fueled by hunger, a group of peasants in Fengyang County, who took the risk of being punished for "running the capitalist road," started a secret contract-production-to-household experiment in their village. The secret was soon revealed to other villages. Under the tacit consent of local authorities, the practice spread to most counties of the province. A similar practice also spontaneously emerged in Sichuan Province, where Zhao Ziyang was then the provincial Party boss.[45]

Nonetheless, during the period 1978 to 1980, almost all the important Party and government documents concerning agricultural policies explicitly prohibited the practice of contract-production-to-household and the return of household farming. The main tone of these documents was to develop a "production responsibility system" and to "consolidate and develop the rural collective economy."[46] The "production responsibility system," according to official description, was predominantly a mechanism through which the reward received was more closely tied to the work performed by the farmer engaging in collective production. Were this guideline strictly followed, the rural reform would have resulted in no more than a better conceived means of formulating contracts among small groups within the production team.

The official guideline, however, turned out to be important only in government documents. As soon as the egalitarian ideology no longer dominated, many local authorities tacitly permitted peasants to experiment with a variety of ways to organize production. Meanwhile, there was a bitter debate within the Party on the "nature" of the contract-production-to-household practice: whether it was consistent with socialist principles.[47] It was not until 1980 when a Party document allowed those "rural production teams with special difficulties" (which accounted for only five percent of total teams) to adopt the practice.

Table 6.2 Average Annual Per Capita Income of Rural Households
(yuan, nominal value)

Year	1978	1980	1985
Per Capita Income	133.57 (100%)	191.33 (100%)	397.60 (100%)
from collective-run business	88.53 (66.30%)	108.37 (56.60%)	33.37 (8.40%)
from household-run business	35.79 (26.80%)	62.55 (32.70%)	322.53 (81.10%)
from other sources	9.25 (6.90%)	20.41 (10.70%)	41.70 (10.50%)

Source: Statistic Bureau of the PRC, *China Statistical Abstract* (1988), T 8.14.

It was not that hard, however, for peasants to discover what was better for them. The rapid spread of the practice went beyond the control of the central authorities, and by the end of 1982, 78 percent of rural production teams had contracted their land to individual households. The progress of rural productivity finally convinced the central authorities which "cat" was more able to catch "mice." Pragmatic consideration of agricultural development overwhelmed the ideological worries about the breaking up of collective farming. The Party's "Number One" document of 1983 fully acknowledged the legitimacy of the household contract system and removed all the restrictions previously imposed on the practice.[48] Most of the more collective forms of the responsibility system had given way to contract-production-to-household by the year of 1983. Table 6.2 shows that the major source of rural households' income switched from collective farming to household farming in the early 1980s.

Similar policy adjustments could be observed in other aspects of the rural economy. In the early stages of rural reform, the government prohibited peasants from a series of productive activities. These included: re-contracting their contracted land to other households, hiring hands to assist in agricultural production, abandoning agricultural activity to specialize in commercial activity, and possessing mechanical transportation tools for commercial purposes. Peasants' spontaneous practices, however, widely broke these restrictions, and the government followed to acknowledge the legitimacy of these practices in 1983.[49] Private initiative also played an important role in institutional changes regarding rural industries. In the 1970s, the commune-brigade enterprises, although not within the direct control of state planning, were officially prohibited from supplying a wide variety of products that might conflict with state planning. In the early 1980s the government removed most of the restrictions but the official policy still restricted these enterprises to the framework of "three locals," i.e., local purchase, local processing, and local marketing.[50] Nevertheless, rural entrepreneurs had largely broken the framework in the early 1980s. For instance, a government report noticed that as early as in 1982, the commodities traded in rural township fairs were no longer restricted to those locally made products, but included those transported from distant regions.[51] In 1984 the authorities removed the policy that restricted peasants' commercial activity to the local rural area and allowed peasants to procure, transport, and market agricultural products between regions and to conduct business in urban areas.[52] The official interpretation of this new policy was to encourage specialization and commercialization in the agricultural sector.[53] After 1985, the government abandoned the restrictions in the form of "three locals" and rural industries began to expand their business to urban areas and even abroad.[54] In the late 1980s, a number of these enterprises developed joint ventures with foreign companies.[55]

In the 1980s the major driving force of the rapid growth of rural industries (see Table 6.3) was peasant entrepreneurs' profit seeking activity. The ownership of rural industries became diversified after 1984. Many newly developed enterprises were peasants' partnerships and individually owned businesses (category II in Table 6.3).

Table 6.3   The Growth of Rural Industries

(I——— township and village enterprises;
 II——— other peasants' enterprises)

Year	Number of Enterprises (millions)		Employment (millions)		Gross Product Value	
	I	II	I	II	I	II
1978	1.50		28			
1980	1.42		30		65.7	
1981	1.34		30		72.9	
1982	1.36		31		85.3	
1983	1.35		32		101.7	
1984	1.65	4.41	38	14	143.3	27.6
1985	1.57	10.65	42	28	198.8	74.4
1986	1.51	13.63	44	35	251.6	102.4
1987	1.58	15.87	47	41	322.1	152.2

Source: *Almanac of China's Economy* (1985), pp. V:19-20, (1986) pp. V:42-43, (1988) pp. V:14-15; K. Griffin ed. *Institutional Reform*, Table 6.1, p. 212.

Meanwhile, the collectively-owned rural enterprises also became more profit-oriented. Originally, communes and production brigades developed their non-agricultural enterprises for financing local community services and subsidizing agricultural production. (This is why these enterprises were called "the commune and brigade enterprises.")[56] A major event of rural administration in the early 1980s was the transformation that replaced the communes with township governments and the production brigades with villages. This transformation significantly reduced the economic-managerial role of the rural administrative bodies. Therefore, rural township and village enterprises became more independent and profit-oriented. For instance, in 1980, of the after-tax profit of these enterprises, 7.7 percent was used for purchasing agricultural machinery. About 7.9 percent went to capital construction on farmland, 3.5 percent was to support poor brigades, and 39.7 percent was to expand production, only 5.7 percent remained for collective welfare. This distribution of profits reflected the widely accepted idea that these enterprises were expected to meet the needs of local administration. During the period from 1985 to 1987, that distribution drastically changed. Of rural industries' after-tax profit, the proportion for purchasing agricultural machinery and supporting poor brigades was eliminated. The proportion for capital construction on farmland declined to only 4.6 percent. The proportion for expanding production rose to about 50 percent, and the proportion for collective welfare increased to around 10 percent.[57]

6.5 An Ever-Growing "Supplementary Role"

Private entrepreneurs also played an important role in changing the institutional environment of the private economy in the urban area. In the early 1980s, after making years of persistent efforts to eliminate the private sector, the government began to adopt a more permissive stance toward individual business in urban areas. The following factors contributed to this policy change.

(a) The urgent pressure of unemployment. The pressure of unemployment among young people was one of the most acute problems facing the government after the Cultural Revolution. During the 1960s to 1970s, Mao sent about 17 million young urban people to the rural area to be "reeducated" through manual labor.[58] By the end of the 1970s, as a part of the general liberalization, a majority of these young people sought to return to their urban hometowns and reunite with their families. To solve the employment problem of a suddenly enlarged young labor force, the government decided in 1980 to develop various ways of stimulating employment, including the support for the growth of the private economy. From 1977 to 1980, more than 28 million people found newly created jobs, most of which were in non-state sectors.[59] A particularly appealing aspect of the policy was that individual businesses could create jobs and absorb surplus labor without an infusion of scarce state funds.

(b) Inadequate supply in service and retail industries. After decades of development biased in favor of heavy industry, urban service and retail industries, mainly state and collectively owned, were in poor conditions. There were the so-called "three major difficulties" for the urban residents at the end of the 1970s: namely the difficulty of finding a restaurant, the difficulty of having clothes made, and the difficulty of obtaining repair services.[60] The development of the private service sector greatly alleviated these problems. About 89 percent of the 5.35 million retail stores, restaurants, and service firms that emerged during the period from 1978 to 1983 were individual businesses. Private retail firms also improved the efficiency of state-owned enterprises by marketing their goods.[61]

(c) Fiscal revenue. Despite the suspicion that tax evasion widely existed among individual business owners, individual enterprises remitted to the state some 13 billion yuan in taxes from 1979 to 1984.[62] This became an important reason for many localities to support the growth of the local private economy. In Shandong Province for instance, one tenth of the provincial budget revenue in 1989 came from the taxes paid by the local private economy, which employed two million people, accounting for about 5 percent of the province's labor force.[63]

In the early 1980s the government adopted the liberal policy toward the private economy to ease short-term pressures. Without a long-term strategy, the evolution of official policies toward the private sector was essentially a process of adjustments to practical needs in the 1980s. These adjustments are a mixture of conscientious reforms and passive concessions to private entrepreneurs' spontaneous activities.

In 1980 when the government was alarmed about the serious situation of urban unemployment, it eased the ban on individual business. Based on a national meeting on the issue, the government promulgated two documents in 1981. One was "The Resolution to Open a Variety of Ways to Solve the Problem of Urban Unemployment," the other was "The Regulations of the Urban Non-agricultural Individual Economy."[64] These documents encouraged unemployed people to open their own "individual businesses." They allowed virtually all the unemployed to apply for the license of "individual business." At the same time, the government imposed a number of restrictions on the "individual businesses." For instance, it designated that individual businesses' purchase of non-planned raw material "should be made on assigned markets"; "all individual firms who purchase from state wholesale resources should strictly comply with the uniform state retail prices." The government prohibited individual businesses from "reselling raw materials for profit, or pushing [or bidding] up price by speculative purchase."[65] The regulation restricted the number of people a firm might hire to two, and the number of apprentices to five. It also banned private wholesale business, and declared "speculation" as illegal. Government policy also constrained the scope of business to cottage handicrafts, retail commerce, and the service and repair trades.[66]

When individual businesses grew, the above restrictions failed to confine private entrepreneurs' activities. The business of some individual firms expanded rapidly to a variety of trades unexpected by the government. In January 1982, concerned about the prevailing "speculation," the government initiated a campaign to attack "the serious crimes in the economic field." The major task of the campaign was to reduce "speculative activities," which included competitive purchase of planned commodities and resale for profit, the resale of imports, exchange of futures, speculatively bidding up prices, and so forth.[67] The administrative organs also made great efforts to ensure "the socialist orientation of individual businesses."[68]

In September 1982, the political report of the Party's Twelfth National Congress stated that the "working people's individual economy" was supposed to play a supplementary role to the publicly owned economy. The report also suggested the government to leave the legitimate activities of private businesses (which were "unimportant" and "supplementary" to the national economy) to "full market coordination."[69] Accordingly, the authorities adjusted policies toward individual business after the congress. In the spring of 1983, the state council issued the "Supplementary Policies on the Urban Non-agricultural Individual Economy." In this document, the government permitted urban individual firms to run wholesale business, transport goods for sale between distant localities, and invest in modern physical capital such as machinery and trucks. The new regulation also expanded the legitimate scope of the "individual business" to transportation, construction, hotels, mining, and manufacturing.[70] Several decrees and rules issued in 1987 further detailed and formalized these policies.[71]

The entrepreneurial growth of the private firms not only pioneered the adjustments of official policy concerning their business scope and operation manner, but also defied the legislative limitation on their firm size. Even in the early 1980s when "individual businesses" embarked on the path of revival, some firms started to challenge the restriction. A well-known case was the private entrepreneur, Mr. Nian Guangjiu, who owned a nationwide business of processing melon seeds and employed hundreds of workers. During the period 1981 to 1987 more than twenty of China's newspapers and magazines presented and discussed Mr. Nian's case.[72] In the mid-1980s, there emerged a number of private firms that owned considerable amounts of capital assets and employed dozens and even hundreds of employees. This sign of "capitalism" sparked a heated debate among economists and policy makers. For example, in 1986 a report published by Guangdong Provincial Academy of Social Sciences expressed worries about the rapid growth of large private enterprises. It described the "adverse influence" of these enterprises on the state plan and the public economy, and the "exploitation of surplus value" within these firms. It blamed the increasing disparity in income distribution and rampant bureaucratic corruption on the unchecked growth of these firms. The report therefore recommended tightening controls over private enterprises.[73]

The official statistical standards defined those private firms with more than eight employees as "private enterprises." After several years' policy debates and official attempts to tighten control, the number of these enterprises continued to grow, despite their employment of more employees than that was legally allowed. By the end of 1986, an official survey showed that the number of such enterprises had reached 60,000 (Table 6.1). In the beginning of 1987, a Party document stipulated perhaps the first written official policy toward these enterprises. Under this policy the government will "allow them [the private enterprises] to exist, reinforce regulations on them, promote what are beneficial and eliminate what are harmful, and guide them gradually to the right path." This de facto official acknowledgment of the existence of "private enterprises," although rather ambiguous, resulted in a boom year for the private enterprises: they grew in number by 93 percent in 1987. A year later, the National People's Congress passed an amendment to the constitution to award private enterprises legal status in the economy. The new law endows private enterprises legal right to exist and protects their legitimate interests.[74] The government also promulgated a temporary bylaw concerning private enterprises in 1988, which defined that private enterprises included proprietorships, partnerships, and corporations. The only private businesses prohibited under the law were finance and armaments. The new law also allowed private enterprises to develop joint ventures with foreign companies. Moreover, the bylaw allowed state-employed scientists and technicians to resign their jobs and open their own businesses.[75] Here, the action of private entrepreneurs again preceded the changes in official policies. For instance, in Fujian Province private businesses by 1988 already accounted for one tenth of the joint-ventures with foreign companies.[76] In 1987, a number of individual business owners were entrepreneurs who were formerly state enterprise employees but had quit their jobs.[77]

Although the official guideline for the private sector was to let it play a supplementary role to the state-owned sector, in some areas the private entrepreneurs developed their business far beyond this stricture. For example, by the end of 1980s, Wenzhou, a city of 6.44 million people in Zhejiang Province, had uniquely developed a local economy with the private sector accounted at least 40 percent of GNP. Free market coordinated about 80 percent of the local economy. The private sector created 1.2 million jobs in the 1980s. The local residents enjoyed a boost in standard of living. In 1989 per capita monetary income of urban inhabitants in the city was 33.25 percent higher than the national averages; and that of the suburban inhabitants was 53.49 percent higher.[78]

6.6 Concluding Comments

To a large extent, private entrepreneurs pioneered China's economic reforms of the 1980s. Driven by their desire for profits, private entrepreneurs defied the existing institutional constraints imposed upon their business and pushed policy makers toward more market-oriented reforms. The process of China's reform in the 1980s was characterized by a mixture of official elite reformers' initiative and private entrepreneurs' spontaneous action to break institutional barriers. In many cases, as illustrated earlier, when private entrepreneurs' activities emerged on a small scale, the official reaction to them tended to be ambiguous or negative. However, when these activities became a prevailing *fait accompli*, official approval followed upon pragmatic considerations and the government made institutional changes to accommodate these activities.

The role of these activities in economic reform echos the "distortion correcting role" of entrepreneurship we dicussed in Section 2.5. In suppressed markets, entrepreneurs get around the official restriction to charge the market clearing prices and therefore correct market distortions. When they seek entry into markets officially closed to them, they are filling the disequilibrium gap instituted by the suppression. The Chinese private entrepreneurs' action to break institutional barriers to free business operation matched all these features of the "distortion-correcting entrepreneurial activity."

This process was by no means smooth and costless. Private entrepreneurs' institutional innovation involved considerable social waste. During China's economic reforms of the 1980s, the government repeatedly launched campaigns to crack down on what it called "economic crimes." To some extent, these campaigns reflected the collision between private entrepreneurs' activities and the existing institutions. Both official efforts to crack down on illegal economic activities and individual entrepreneurs' attempts to escape official policing generated social tension and extra cost to both society and the individuals. Meanwhile, the unstable official policy and ambiguous legal framework created the danger of causing social cynicism toward law and order. This cynicism might in turn induce entrepreneurs to behave with little regard for the legitimacy of their actions. It also makes the development of a "well-ordered" market economy more difficult. Moreover, with expectation for an uncertain market environment, entrepreneurs tended to do their business myopically by holding back important investment in capital goods, technology, goodwill and reputation. This myopic behavior might tar the image of private businesses and invite social hostility toward entrepreneurs. Among other causes, the negative impact of interactions between official policies and private entrepreneurship accounts for the slowdown if not the retreat of China's economic reform after the Tiananmen Event in 1989.

NOTES

1. *On Questions of the Party History--Resolution on Certain Questions in the History of the CPC Since the Founding of the People's Republic of China* (a party document adopted by the Sixth Plenum of the Eleventh Central Committee of the CPC on June 27, 1981), Liu and Wu ed., op. cit., Appendix III, p. 610.

2. Dong Furen, "*Jingji Jizhi he Suoyouzhi de Gaige*"("The Reform of Economic Mechanism and Ownership"), *Jingji Yanjiu* (Economic Research), No. 7, 1988, p. 27.

3. Perkins, Dwight, "Reforming China's Economic System," op. cit. pp. 603-610.

4. Yearbook Editorial Board, *Zhong Gong Nianjian (Yearbook on Chinese Communism) 1989*, Taipei, Taiwan: The Institute for the Study of Chinese Communist Problems, 1989, p. IV:37.

5. Yearbook Editorial Board, op. cit., p. IV:37.

6. Almanac Editorial Board, *Zhongguo Jingji Nianjian* (Almanac of China's Economy), Beijing: Publisher of Beijing Journal of Economic Management, 1988, pp. XI:158-159.

7. Almanac Editorial Board, *Almanac of China's Economy (1984)*, p. IV: 52.

8. See the note in Table 6.1 for the definition of "private enterprises."

9. *Renmin Ribao* (People's Daily), 14 Aug 1989, p. 3.

10. Almanac Editorial Board, *Almanac of China's Economy (1988)*, p. XI 158; Statistical Bureau of the People's Republic of China, *China Statistical Abstract*, New York: Praeger Publishers, 1989, T 2.3.

11. *Renmin Ribao (People's Daily)*, 24 Dec. 1988, p. 3. The investigation was conducted by the Shanghai Research Society of Economic Reform.

12. See Section 5.1 for the meaning of "walking on two legs."

13. Almanac Editorial Board, *Almanac of China's Economy (1985)*, pp. V:19-20.

14. According to Almanac Editorial Board, *Almanac of China's Economy (1985)*, p. V:20, (1986), p. V:42, (1988), p. V:14.

15. Calculated according to Griffin, K. ed., *Institutional Reform and Economic Development in the Chinese Countryside*, New York: M.E. Sharpe, Armonk, 1984, Table 6.2, p. 213, and Statistical Bureau of the PRC, *China Statistical Abstract (1989)*, Table 3.19, p. 37.

16. *Renmin Ribao (People's Daily)*, 11 May 1990, p. 1, 21 May 1990, p. 3.

17. The ratio in 1978 is estimated according to Griffin, loc. cit., Table 6.1, p. 212, and Statistical Bureau of the PRC, *China Statistical Abstract (1988)*, T 1.6, p. 7. The ratio in 1989 was reported by the State Council of China, *Renmin Ribao (People's Daily)*, 12 May 1990, p. 1.

18. Almanac Editorial Board, *Almanac of China's Economy (1988)*, p. V:14, Statistical Bureau of the PRC, *China Statistical Abstract*, T 2.4, p. 17.

19. *Renmin Ribao (People's Daily)*, 16 Jan 1991, p. 3.

20. *Renmin Ribao (People's Daily)*, 28 Feb 1990, p. 3.

21. *Renmin Ribao (People's Daily)*, 2 April 1990, p. 3, 6 June 1990, p. 3.

22. *Renmin Ribao (People's Daily)*, 6 June 1990, p. 3.

23. For example see the Central Committee of the Communist Party of China, "Communique of the Third Plenary Session of the Eleventh Central Committee of the CPC," appendix of Liu, S. and Q. Wu, op. cit, pp. 564-77.

24. *Hongqi (Red Flag)*, No. 16 (23 Nov. 23, 1967), pp. 18-29.

25. See Chang, D.W., *China Under Deng Xiaoping*, New York: St. Martin's Press, 1988, pp. 40-42 for a detailed description of the discussion on truth criterion.

26. See Harding, Harry, *China's Second Revolution: Reform after Mao*, Washington, D.C.: The Brookings Institution, 1987, pp. 11-20 and pp. 78-83 for a more detailed description of the differences between the radical reformers and the moderate reformers.

27. *Renmin Ribao (People's Daily)*, 3 December, 1982.

28. Appendix of Liu, S. and Q. Wu ed, op. cit. pp. 564-77.]

29. Chen Yun, "Economic Conditions and the Lessons of Experience," December 1980, in *San Zhong Quanhui yilai Zhongyao Wenxian Xuanji (Selection of Important Documents since the Third Plenary*, Jilin, China: People's Publishing House, 1982, pp. 601-07.

30. Liu, S. and Q. Wu ed. *China's Socialist Economy*, appendix, p. 630.

31. See Hu Yaobang, "Create a New Situation in All Fields of Socialist Modernization," in *The Twelfth National Congress of the CPC*, Beijing: Foreign Languages Press, 1982, pp. 1-85.

32. See Wu Jinglian and Zhao Renwei, "The Dual Pricing System in China's Industry," *Journal of Comparative Economics*, No. 11, 1987, pp. 309-318, for a description of the evolution of the dual pricing system.

33. The Central Committee of the CPC, "Decision of the Central Committee of the CPC on Reform of the Economic Structure," in *Xuexi Cailiao (Documents for Study)*, Shanghai: Jiefang Ribao Press, Oct. 1984, pp. 2-23.

34. Zhao Ziyang, "The Report on the 13th National Congress of the CPC," *Renmin Ribao (People's Daily)*, 4 November 1987, p. 2.

35. Ibid. p. 2.

36. The 1984 "Decision" stipulated: "Under our socialist conditions, neither labor power nor land, mines, banks, railways and all other state-owned enterprises and resources are commodities." [Liu, S. and Q. Wu ed. op. cit. appendix, p. 682.]

37. Premier Li Peng, in his report at the National People's Congress in April 1990, re-affirmed the necessity of mandatory central planning concerning "the production and transaction of those important products that are related to the national economy and people's livelihood." "[L]arge and medium-sized state owned enterprises should be subject to state mandatory plans or guiding plans, collective economy to guiding plans or market coordination, and individual, private, and foreign enterprises to market coordination." Li also stated the goal of reform as the establishment of "a management system and economic mechanism combining planned economy and market coordination." [Li Peng, "Report on the Third Meeting of the 7th National People's Congress," *Renmin Ribao (People's Daily)*, 6 April 1990, p. 2.]

38. Zhao Ziyang, "The Report on the 13th National Congress of the CPC," *Renmin Ribao (People's Daily)*, 4 Nov. 1987, p. 1.

39. Ibid, p. 2.

40. Xinhua News Agency, 14 September 1986, in *Foreign Broadcasting Information Service*, 16 September, 1986, pp. B 1-3.

41. Jiang Zemin's speech on the anniversary of the founding of the PRC, *Renmin Ribao (People's Daily)*, 30 Sept. 1989, p. 1.

42. Almanac Editorial Board, *Almanac of China's Economy (1981)*, p. IV:13.

43. Yang Tianshu, "*Shui Gai Ling Nongcun Gaige de Tian Gong* (Who Should be Awarded for Leading the Rural Reform)?" *Zhongguo Zhi Chun (China Spring)* [Flushing, New York], No. 71 (April 1989), pp. 29-32.

44. Almanac Editorial Board, *Almanac of China's Economy (1981)*, p. III 62.

45. Yang Tianshu, op. cit. pp. 30-31.

46. Almanac Editorial Board, *Almanac of China's Economy (1981)*, pp. IV:12-14; Yearbook Editorial Board, *Yearbook on Chinese Communism (1989)*, pp. IV:36-37.

47. Zhou Qiren (a former researcher of China's Research Institute of Rural Development)'s speech on rural reform, *Zhongguo Zhi Chun (China Spring)*, no. 65, Oct. 1988, pp. 22-25.

48. Yearbook Editorial Board, *Yearbook on Chinese Communism (1989)*, pp. IV:36-37.

49. Ibid. p. IV:37.

50. Enos, J.L. "Commune- and Brigade-run Industries in Rural China," in K. Griffin ed., *Institutional Reform and Economic Development in the Chinese Countryside*, pp. 240-41.

51. Almanac Editorial Board, *Almanac of China's Economy* (1983), p. IV:185.

52. Almanac Editorial Board, *Almanac of China's Economy (1985)*, p. IV:42.

53. Yu Guoyao, "*Zhongguo Nongcun Jingji Gaige de Shenhua he Fazhan*" ("The Deepening and Development of Economic Reform in China's Rural Area"), in Almanac Editorial Board, *Almanac of China's Economy (1981)*, pp. II:5-6.

54. Almanac Editorial Board, *Almanac of China's Economy* (1985), p. V:20.

55. *Renmin Ribao (People's Daily)*, 21 May 1990, p. 3.

56. Xue Muqiao, "*Woguo Shengchan Ziliao Suoyouzhi de Yanbian*" ("The Evolution of the Ownership of Production Means in China"),

Jingji Yanjiu (Economic Research) [Beijing, China], No. 2 (1982), pp. 18-19.

57. Calculated according to Statistical Bureau of the PRC, *China Rural Statistics 1988*, New York: Praeger, 1990, Table 6.2, p. 126.

58. Rosen, Stanley, "The Private Economy," *Chinese Economic Studies*, Vol. XXI, No.1 (1987), pp. 3-9.

59. Almanac Editorial Board, *Almanac of China's Economy (1981)*, pp. IV:179.

60. Almanac Editorial Board, *Almanac of China's Economy (1982)*, p. V:416.

61. Almanac Editorial Board, *Almanac of China's Economy (1984)*, p. IV:52.

62. Zhu Qingfang, "On the Evolution and Changes of the Individual Economy," *Chinese Economic Studies*, Vol. 21, no.2, Winter 1987-88, pp. 100-176.

63. *Renmin Ribao (People's Daily)*, 19 May 1990, p. 3, Statistical Bureau of Shangdong Province, *Shandong Tongji Nianjian (Statistical Almanac of Shandong)*, Beijing: China Statistics Press 1989, p. 355.

64. Almanac Editorial Board, *Almanac of China's Economy (1982)*, p. V:416.

65. Commercial Department et al, "Announcement on Raw Material Supply of Urban Individual Business (22 June 1981)," Almanac Editorial Board, *Almanac of China's Economy (1982)*, p. III:91.

66. State Council, "Policies on Urban Non-agricultural Individual Business (7 July 1981)," Almanac Editorial Board, *Almanac of China's Economy (1982)*, p. III:92.

67. Gong Xiaolan, "China's Commerce Regulation," Almanac Editorial Board, *Almanac of China's Economy* (1983), p. IV:185.

68. Almanac Editorial Board, *Almanac of China's Economy (1983)*, p. IV:348.

69. Hu Yaobang, "Create a New Situation in All Fields of Socialist Modernization," in *The 12th National Congress of the CPC*, Beijing: Foreign Languages Press, 1982, pp. 1-85.

70. Almanac Editorial Board, *Almanac of China's Economy (1984)*, p. IX:55.

71. Almanac Editorial Board, *Almanac of China's Economy (1988)*, p. IX:72-73.

72. Stanley Rosen, "The Private Economy," *Chinese Economic Studies*, Vol. 21, no.1, 1987, p. 7.

73. Mo Zhen, "Tighten Control over Big Labor-Hiring Households in Rural Areas," *Chinese Economic Studies*, Vol. 21 no.2, 1987, pp. 90-95.

74. Almanac Editorial Board, *Almanac of China's Economy (1988)*, p. XI:157.

75. "The PRC Temporary Bylaw of the Private Enterprises," *Renmin Ribao (People's Daily)*, 30 June 1988, p. 3.

76. Almanac Editorial Board, *Almanac of China's Economy (1989)*, p. X:152.

77. Almanac Editorial Board, *Almanac of China's Economy (1988)*, p. XI:159.

78. *Renmin Ribao (People's Daily)*, 29 May 1990, p. 3, 28 May 1991, p. 3.

CHAPTER 7

FORTUNE IN
A SEMI-MARKET ECONOMY

7.1 Introduction

While achieving rapid economic growth in the 1980s, China also encountered a series of chaotic consequences of economic reform. One source of these chaotic consequences can be traced to the widespread rent-seeking activities present in the economy.

As defined in Chapter 3, there are two kinds of rent-seeking activities in a centrally-planned economy. "Vertical rent seeking" refers to the efforts of enterprise managers to bargain for favorable economic treatment with their supervisory authorities along the planning hierarchy. "Horizontal rent seeking" involves the illicit trade of goods and services that are in shortage for contrived benefits. This chapter examines the impact of these two kinds of rent-seeking activities on economic reform.

The next section describes the chaotic aspects of the reform. In particular, we will discuss the three major problems of Chinese economy in the late 1980s: the runaway inflation, the rising economic crimes, and the worsening inequality of income distribution. Section 7.3 explore the source of inflationary pressure — the deteriorating state budget conditions. It shows that the state budget problem was mainly a result of the low efficiency of the state-owned sector and the drain of government funds. These two phenomena were closely related to vertical rent seeking of localities and state-owned enterprises. Section 7.4 views the rampant economic crimes in the 1980s as a consequence of horizontal rent seeking conducted by entrepreneurs and corrupt bureaucrats. Behind the phenomenon, there were institutional changes that favored the growth of illegal horizontal rent-seeking activities. The last section comments on these activities using the theoretical concepts developed in the first three chapters of the book.

7.2 The Road to Tiananmen

In October 1987, the former Party General Secretary Zhao Ziyang forecast confidently that only thirty percent of the economy would remain centrally-planned in two or three years, compared with the situation nine years earlier of almost one hundred percent central planning and the present percentage of fifty.[1] He also predicted a year later that the full success of price reform could be attained in about five years.[2] After that, however, the reform encountered serious economic difficulties and social unrest, which led to the tragic event of Tiananmen Square and the ejection of Zhao in 1989. The most acute problems by the end of the 1980s were the runaway inflation, social disorders that resulted from rampant economic crimes, and the worsening inequality of income distribution.

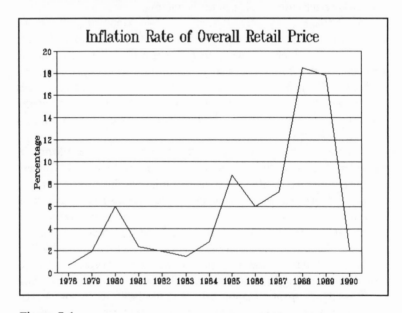

Figure 7.1
Source: *China Trade and Price Statistics* 1988, T 2.7; State Statistical Bureau's annual reports of 1989 and 1990.

The pressure of inflation.

Inflation pressure had plagued China's economy ever since the country had embarked on the path of economic reform (Figure 7.1). This prompted the initial drive for the massive student demonstration in 1989, which partially represented the popular anger against increasing living costs and bureaucratic corruption. In Figure 7.1 it is possible to see that the two years in which the inflation rate steeply increased coincided with two important political events: The rise and crackdown of two nationwide student demonstrations and the ejection of two former Party general secretaries, Hu Yaobang and Zhao Ziyang in 1987 and 1989 respectively. Consequently, the threat of hyperinflation to social stability made the government hold back the much needed price reform and delay other reform schemes in 1988 and 1989 (See more detailed accounts about the setback of the reform below).

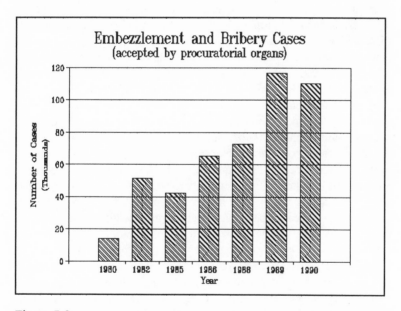

Figure 7.2
Source: *P.R. China Yearbook*; *Procuratorial Yearbook of China*; *Renmin Ribao (People's Daily)*'s related reports. (The number of 1980 includes all sorts of economic crimes).

Social disorders and increasing economic crimes.

In addition to inflation, bureaucratic corruption was another immediate threat to social stability.[3] Figure 7.2 illustrates the increase of economic crimes in the 1980s. Of these crimes, corruption and bribery composed the major part. For instance, 79.9 percent of the total number of economic crimes filed and prosecuted in 1986 were corruption and bribery cases, and 51 percent of the criminals involved in these cases were state personnel, including high ranking officials.[4] In 1982, about eighty to ninety million yuan was retrieved when procuratorial organs prosecuted embezzlement and bribery cases, constituting approximately ten times of the amount of money retrieved in 1980. In 1989 and 1990, this number significantly increased to 482.86 million and 810 million yuan respectively.[5]

In the 1980s, the government launched waves of campaigns against economic crimes. Beginning in 1980, economic jurisdiction was strengthened and economic tribunals at all levels of the People's court were established to curb economic crimes and to solve economic disputes.[6] As shown in Figure 7.3, the main task of China's judicial administration was converted to the handling of economic cases in the mid-1980s. Of the criminal charges, about 20 percent cases involved economic crimes. In March 1982, the Fifth National Congress Standing Committee adopted a decision to punish severely economic crimes. By the end of 1985, courts in China had tried 183,000 cases of economic crimes, punishing 224,000 offenders.[7]

The effects of the official crackdown on economic crimes, however, were limited. For example, in the early 1980s, a number of state organs, institutions, and enterprises "engaged in speculating and smuggling, and disturbing the monetary market."[8] By 1985, 320,000 bureaucracy-related corporations emerged nationwide. Most of these corporations were known as "briefcase corporations" engaging in speculative business without financial capital, production equipment, or even fixed offices. After one year of the intensified crackdown started by the government, the number of such corporations went down to 180,000. However, when the campaign was over in the period from 1987 to September 1988, the number of these corporations soon rebounded to 295,000.[9] Many of these newly developed corporations were run by state organs, which profiteered by utilizing monopolistic administrative powers. For instance, some state organs, whose duty was to allocate foreign exchange quotas among state import and export enterprises, retained the scarce currency for the business of their own companies. Some state wholesale institutions, which were supposed to supply raw materials at planned prices to state enterprises, abused their power and sold these materials at higher market prices for profit. In addition, some government branches in charge of issuing import permits and licenses sold these certificates to the highest bidders.[10]

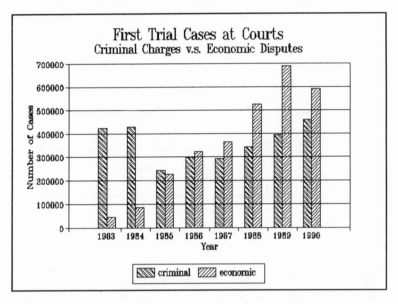

Figure 7.3
Source: *P.R. China Yearbook*, 1987, 1988; *Renmin Ribao (People's Daily)*, 13 April 1991, p. 4.

Increased social inequality.

Income inequality increased sharply in the late 1980s. An empirical study by Zhang and Tam shows that in the 1980s inequality increased in both the urban and rural areas (see Figure 7.4).[11] The study applies the technique of the General Lorenz Curve, which is obtained by multiplying the values of a Lorenz curve by the population's mean income. According to this study, the rise in the mean income had more than compensated the increase of inequality before 1985. After 1985, however, real income did not increase sufficiently to do so.

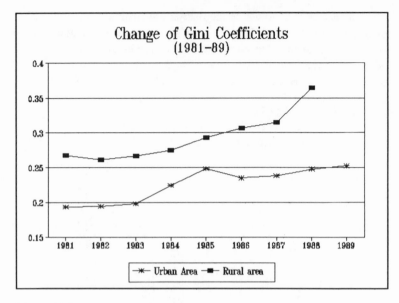

Figure 7.4
Source: Zhang and Tam, op. cit. Gini coefficients were calculated on deflated nominal per capita income.

It seemed that an increasing proportion of the urban population was worse off absolutely in the late 1980s. According to official surveys, the percentage of urban families whose real income declined was 21 percent in 1987, 34.9 percent in 1988, and 35.8 percent in 1989.[12]

An important aspect of inequality was the "unfair" distribution that resulted from the highly distorted market conditions. As General Secretary Jiang Zemin pointed out, "There are many problems, some are serious problems, in the contemporary income distribution system. On the one hand, among the employees who live on wage/salary incomes in (state-owned) enterprises, nonprofit institutions, and administrations, the problem of egalitarian distribution has not yet been solved, and even has grown in some localities, departments, and fields. On the other hand, however, there has emerged new social inequality due to the serious disparity in income distribution. This is mainly reflected by the sharp gap between the incomes of wage/salary earners such as the majority of workers, cadres, and intellectuals, and the incomes of those people who are staff of non-productive corporations, who engage in 'second careers', and, especially, who own and run private business or work as individual laborers. This problem has aroused serious concerns in our society and caused resentment among the working people. Social inequality in distribution is not only an economic problem, but also a social and political problem."[13]

As shown in Figure 7.5, the average nominal wage of state employees was not only lower than that of employees in the "other" category (i.e., sectors other than state-owned and collective-owned), but also growing at a much slower rate than in the latter. From 1986 to 1990, the average annual growth rate of real wage was 2.6 percent for state-owned employees and 1.0 percent for collective enterprise employees. Contrarily, the employees in the "other" category saw a 4.7 percent annual growth of their wages in the period.[14] In fact, the real average wage of the state employees declined by 0.7 percent in 1988.[15]

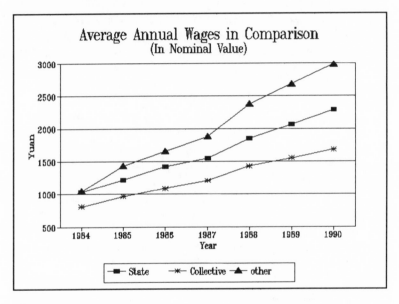

Figure 7.5
Source: *China Statistical Abstract*, 1989, T 8.6; *China Social Statistics* (1986), New York: Praeger, 1989, T 61. *Zhongguo Tongji Nianjian* (Statistical Yearbook of China), 1991, p. 120.
Note: the wages are in nominal value.

The contrasts between the incomes of wage earners and non-wage earners were more impressive, as expressed in the previous quotation from Jiang. For example, in Wenzhou, a city of 6,440,000 people in Zhejiang Province where at least 40 percent of the local economy is private, per capita monetary income of urban inhabitants in 1989 was 33.25 percent higher than the national averages, and that of rural inhabitants was 53.49 percent higher.[16]

There was also a significant regional disparity in income distribution because economic reform developed unevenly between localities. An important principle of China's economic reform has been the concept of *shidian*, which means that reform schemes should be first adopted experimentally in selected regions before they are implemented nationwide.

In 1981, the State Council chose the title of "Economic Institution Reform Experimental City"(EIRE cities) as a label for certain cities, and authorized these cities to carry out experimental reforms in a more flexible framework.[17] The number of EIRE cities was 72 by the end of 1988. Meanwhile, two southern coastal provinces, Guangdong and Fujian, were selected as experimental provinces for economic reform in the early 1980s.

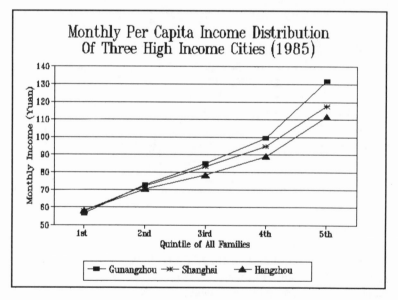

Figure 7.6
Source: *China Social Statistics* 1986, T 4.10.

In 1987, the per worker wage-profit ratio (i.e., the average wage as a ratio to pretax profit per worker) was 1:1.5 for China's 382 cities. The 72 EIRE cities, however, had a per worker wage-profit ratio of 1:1.05, suggesting that these cities retained a higher proportion of per worker business earnings as wages. This dichotomy was even sharper between Shanghai, the largest industrial city in China that was under relatively strict central planning in the 1980s, and Guangzhou, the capital of Guangdong Province: the ratio was 1:2.32 for Shanghai and 1:1.01 for Guangzhou. This indicates that Guangzhou, a city enjoying more economic autonomy, distributed a much larger share of per worker business earnings to wages.[18]

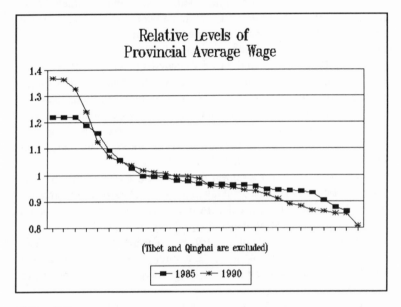

Figure 7.7
Source: *Zhongguo Tongji Nianjian* (Statistical Yearbook of China), 1991, T 4-36, p. 132.
Note:
a. The relative wage level was the provincial average wage divided by the national average wage.
b. The state employees in remote areas such as Xizang (Tibet) and Qinghai receive higher average wages as the result of a government policy to encourage Chinese workers to work there.

Figure 7.6 shows that, compared with the cities with the second and the third highest average incomes in 1985, Guangzhou had a more unequal income distribution. This may suggest the effects of more advanced reforms in Guangzhou. Under the policy of *shidian,* the 1980s saw an increasing income gap between the residents of rich provinces and the residents of poor provinces. Figure 7.7 shows that the differences in average wages among different provinces increased significantly in the decade.

The slowdown and the setback of the reform.

The above consequences of reform led to the slowdown and setback of economic reform in the 1980s, especially in the late 1980s. By the end of 1987, rationing for grain and cooking oil was extended to other products like pork, eggs, and sugar in major cities. In July 1988, the government imposed a partial price freeze because of a 13-percent inflation rate in the first six months of the year.[19]

The second half of the 1988 was a critical period of China's economic reform. November 1, 1988 was supposed to be the date for China to implement its Law of Bankruptcy. It was estimated that with the implementation of the law, at least 300,000 state-owned enterprises would face bankruptcy, and thousands of workers would lose their jobs.[20] In August 1988, the Political Bureau of the CPC passed a comprehensive wage-price reform proposal, which intended to increase prices of a number of industrial raw materials and agricultural products in 1989. It also announced that in the next five years China would move to a price system in which the prices of most goods and services would be freely set by market forces.[21] During the meeting, then General Secretary Zhao Ziyang told a foreign visitor that China was about to "storm fortifications [to clear way] for a comprehensive reform."[22]

This ambitious proposal was soon shelved due to the serious macroeconomic situation. As early as August, China's central bank, the People's Bank, warned that the financial situation was "extraordinarily serious." It reported that compared with the first six months of 1987, the currency in circulation had increased by 35.9 percent and savings deposits had declined by 6.2 percent in the first six months of 1988. This resulted in the panic purchase of goods that were in shortage in major cities and the central bank lost control of the speedy growth of industrial loans.[23] In August and September, the whole country witnessed panic purchases and price hikes.[24] In October, the State

Council, led by Premier Li Peng, held a series of emergency meetings in order to impose price ceilings on a number of raw material goods. These meetings also attempted to devise a unified state plan for the supply of important products. The meetings decided issues on investigation and purge of commercial corporations and designed the plans to crack down those corporations' "speculative activities." The government decided to tighten the money supply and the governmental budget expenses. It was announced that economic reform would slow down and the measures of retrenchment would be implemented during a two-year rectification period.[25] In January 1989, the People's Bank significantly raised the interest rate and started to peg the rate to the inflation rate for some long term deposits.[26]

After the end of the student movement and the ejection of former General Secretary Zhao Ziyang in the spring of 1989, the government intensified the retrenchment efforts. In November 1989, the Party decided to extend the rectification for at least three more years. Meanwhile, it resolved to abandon the dual price system in favor of the traditional planned price system. The Party also vowed to expand the central government's financial capacity by taking measures to reduce extra-budget funds. An important policy was to restrict the business scope of township and village enterprises and to improve taxation on the private sector and rural industries. The crackdown on economic crimes became a major focus of government policy.[27]

The chaotic aspects of the reform reflected the institutional features of the Chinese economy in transition from central planning to a market economy. In such an economy, there are plenty of opportunities for rent-seeking activities, which waste scarce resources. The rent-seeking competition in the 1980s' was closely related to the source of the previously-mentioned three problems, namely the runaway inflation, social disorders due to economic crimes, and the worsening inequality of income distribution. The major source for the unprecedented pressure of hyperinflation in the 1980s was the growing government's budget deficit. The lack of financial intermediaries determined that the major means available to the government for it to finance the deficit was to print money.[28]

7.3 Loopholes in Contract Responsibility

The pre-reform Chinese economy was a centrally planned economy characterized by a hierarchical decision-making structure and ill-defined public ownership. As some economists of comparative economic systems have identified, the institutional features of such an economy would deprive enterprises of the incentive to improve efficiency through innovation. Instead, enterprises would have an insatiable desire to expand their production capacity by seeking centrally assigned capital resources.[29] Kornai calls this phenomenon "expansion fever" and "investment hunger."[30] In the pre-reform Chinese economy, the "expansion fever" and "investment hunger" of localities and enterprises were partially counterbalanced by a highly centralized management structure. This structure, however, was greatly weakened in China's economy of the 1980s.

The basic idea of China's economic reform concerning the state-owned sector involved separation of ownership and management.[31] This meant the delegation of decision-making power to business managers without abolishing state ownership of the means of production. The aim was to invigorate state-owned enterprises, namely, to encourage entrepreneurship in these enterprises without changing their socialist nature.

During the 1980s, the autonomy of the state-owned industrial enterprises greatly increased, especially after the Party recognized in its *Decision on Reform* in 1984 that the key to reform was invigorating enterprises.[32] Two major reform schemes were introduced in 1983 and 1984. One was the so-called "*li gai shui*" (taxes-for-profits), which sought to dismantle the system where all profits after subtracting a small retained portion for the enterprise were simply returned to the state. The reform aims to adopt a corporate profit tax that would allow substantial retained earnings. By 1986, almost all enterprise profits were taxed (although not at a uniform rate), instead of being remitted to the government. Another was the so-called "*bo gai dai*" (loans-for-grants), which strove to move away from the provision of investment funds on a grant basis from the government budget toward the allocation of working capital and investment funds through the banking system.[33] In 1984, the central government announced a series of measures to enlarge state enterprises' autonomy. Different forms of "management contracts" or "contracted managerial responsibility" systems[34] were applied to most state enterprises.[35] According to an official of the State Council, 90 percent of the industrial and commercial enterprises were covered by the contracted managerial responsibility system in 1988.[36] Although these reforms did not totally overcome many drawbacks of the old system with respect to bureaucratic involvement in enterprise decision making, they greatly changed the operational environment of the state enterprises. With the reforms, the government had hardened enterprise budget constraints and made enterprise behavior more market-oriented. However, when enterprise managers were delegated more decision-making authority over state-owned resources, the potential for abusing the use of business funds, especially the investment funds and the wages/fringe benefit funds, immediately increased.

The new norms to harness the behavior of the enterprises were a variety of contract management responsibility systems, which were designed to harden the budget constraints of the enterprises and provide a solution to the problem of ill-defined ownership. A similar principle was also applied to the center-locality relationship. Traditionally, major taxes were collected by local governments. The local governments then remitted a certain portion of tax revenue to the central government.

A major reform regarding the center-local relationship was the so-called "*fen zao chi fan*" (eating in separate canteens), which changed the previously highly centralized budget system to a system featuring stratified management with contractual responsibilities at each level. The revenue-sharing contracts between the central and local governments featured a quota arrangement. Those contracts fixed revenue-sharing ratios between the center and the localities, or even fixed an annual lump sum handover to the Central Government for a several-year period. After meeting the handover quota, the local government would retain the rest. Under this framework, the local governments became financially independent and able to decide the uses of their funds without approval from higher authorities.[37] The practice started in two southern provinces, Guangdong and Fujian, in 1980. In the late 1980s, the "*fen zao chi fan*" practice spread to most of the other provinces and localities.

To a certain extent, these contract responsibility systems hardened the budget constraints of state-owned enterprises and the localities while delegating autonomy to their managers. Nevertheless, the new systems also created an institutional environment in which local governments had stronger incentives and more opportunities of intervention into enterprise decision-making.

The tax-for-profit reform in 1983 and 1984 was viewed as a scheme of partially privatizing property rights at the enterprise level. It was expected that when the relationship of state-owned enterprises to the state was reduced to the simple submission of taxes, the enterprises would behave more like private firms characterized by financial independence and hard budget constraints. In the Chinese economy of the 1980s, however, market distortions were numerous and the price system continued to producing incorrect signals. The distorted profits under a uniform tax rate would leave many actually efficient enterprises suffering business losses and would encourage production expansion in the wrong sectors. The government therefore introduced an array of "corrective taxes" to compensate for profit distortions that resulted from the distorted price system and other factors that lay beyond the control of business management. [In China, the factors that are beyond the control of management are called *keguan tiaojian* (objective conditions), and the factors that on the responsibility of management are labeled *zhuguan tiaojian* (subjective conditions)].

This consideration was especially important for local governments. Since these "objective conditions" existed, it was quite possible that some enterprises crucial to the local economy might not make a profit. Therefore, in the local government's point of view, it was necessary to subsidize these enterprises in order to maintain local economic development. Consequently, the redistribution of local business income in favor of these enterprises became an important function of the local government. One way to accomplish this was to manipulate the effective tax rates of the enterprises. Although the statutory tax rates were set by the central government, the local authorities were able to set the effective tax rates by deciding each enterprise's tax base during contract negotiations. Since effective tax rates were tailored to the profit of each enterprise, the determination of the direction and the amount of compensation remained an arbitrary process of negotiation between bureaucrats and managers.[38]

In addition to this "soft taxation" scheme, the local government possessed other means to redistribute business incomes. One was the charge of administrative levies on the retained profits of enterprises in the name of "concentration of funds" by local industrial bureaus or other administrative organs. There were also the "interest free loan" or "subsidized interest loan" (the negative-interest loan) arranged by local governments through financial institutions.[39] The latter solution was especially risky in the sense of the money supply. This was because in

China the credit plan of the banking system was accommodative to the overall planning process and developed "from bottom up": Local authorities submitted their credit needs, which then became the subject of negotiations with the central government.[40] With these means to redistribute business incomes, the local government played a vital role in influencing the behavior of enterprises. The following are some consequences of the system.

The low efficiency of state-owned enterprises.

For managers of state-owned enterprises, bargaining for favorable financial treatment on the plea of "objective conditions" became an attractive rent-seeking alternative to seeking profits through managerial efforts. A proportion of entrepreneurial resources were thus wasted in unproductive uses. As observed by Walder, there were several effective strategies used by managers to bargain for favorable taxation and financial treatment. The first one was the traditional hoarding behavior: Managers reserved production capacity in fulfilling the tax quota to avoid a rise of the quota in the next contract period. The second strategy was the disguise of poor management by fawning on the labor force through payments and benefit increase. The third measure was the use of the state plan to argue for business priority. Finally, managers also demand renovative investment by complaining about antiquated equipment. On the other hand, the existence of "objective conditions," the notion that drove these bargaining strategies, also justified the responsibility of the local authorities to monitor and intervene extensively in enterprise management and to redistribute income among the enterprises. Therefore, they handled the managerial contracts with discretion.[41]

Because of this interaction that occurred between enterprises and governmental authorities, managers of state-owned enterprises devoted much of their efforts to unproductive uses. Largely because of this, the state-owned sector was trapped in a state of low efficiency in the 1980s, which ran in sharp contrast to the blossoming private and cooperative economy.[42] In his report to the Third Plenary of the Seventh National People's Congress, Premier Li Peng admitted that "the low efficiency of industrial enterprises is the crux of many current difficulties."[43]

Table 7.1   Economic Efficiency of State-Owned Industrial Enterprises

Year	Average Days for the Circulation of Target Circulating Fund (1)	Tax & Profit (Billion Yuan) (2)	Gross Output (Billion Yuan) (3)	(2) as a Ratio to (3) % (4)
1965	74.8	n.a.	n.a.	30.00
1979	n.a.	n.a.	n.a.	25.00
1982	110.0	n.a.	n.a.	24.10
1985	101.8	119.5	630.20	18.97
1986	109.1	119.3	697.10	17.11
1987	105.4	130.7	825.00	15.84
1988	97.0	155.8	1024.00	15.21
1989	108.0	155.9	1061.89	14.68
1990	127.0	127.1	1092.68	11.63

Source: State Statistical Bureau's Statistical Communique on China's Economic and Social Development, 1986 to 1989; *Almanac of China's Economy* 1983, 1980.

Table 7.1 shows that during the 1980s the state-owned sector failed to resume the speed of circulation of the "target circulating funds" to the level that existed in 1965, the year before the chaotic period of the Cultural Revolution. The circulation of the "target circulating funds" slowed down significantly in 1988 and 1990. Also, as taxes and profits grew at a much slower rate than the gross output value, the ratio of taxes and profits to gross output value fell considerably.

The low efficiency of state-owned enterprises became a heavy burden on the state budget, because state-owned enterprises occupied a decisive position in the calculation of the state budget. For example, in 1988, tax revenues from state-owned enterprises were about 145 billion yuan, constituting more than 60 percent of total tax revenue. Besides, the profit submitted by state-owned enterprises contributed

4.87 billion yuan to state budget revenues.[44] In the meantime, the government spent 44.58 billion yuan to subsidize state-owned enterprises.[45] The subsidy for the state-owned sector's business losses steadily increased from 1986 to 1989 (Figure 7.8). It also accounted for the major source of the state budget deficit (Table 7.2).

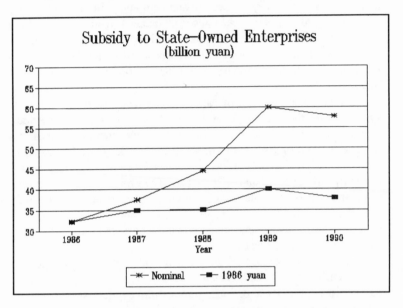

Figure 7.8
Source: Wang Binqian (China's Minister of the State Budget Department), "Reports on State Budget," 1986 to 1991, *Renmin Ribao (People's Daily)*.

Table 7.2 Subsidy to State-Owned Enterprises
as Ratio to State Budget Deficit

1986	1987	1988	1989	1990
1.52	1.31	1.31	1.62	1.14

Source: ibid.

The drain of state revenues.

The contract responsibility system created collaboration between the local government and enterprises against the central government's efforts to control investment and consumption funds. On the one hand, the capacity of local governments to keep resources within their own areas increased as they gained greater autonomy in the 1980s. By manipulating the effective tax rates and financial treatment toward the local enterprises, local governments could help the enterprises retain a larger portion of their profit and share the surplus with the enterprises through the latter's "voluntary" contributions or "apportionment" for local projects.[46]

On the other hand, the management contracts and revenue sharing system made the central government's fiscal policy impotent. Since earnings above the contracted quota were either retained or taxed at a lower rate, this contributed to a pro-cyclical aggregate demand element, that is, taxes as a proportion of national income declined as the economy got heated, and vice versa. Therefore, when the central government perceived the need to control aggregate demand, the only alternatives available to it were to resort to administrative methods to suppress capital investment, to cut down the consumption fund, and to close extra-budget projects.[47]

In the 1980s, the central government had to impose three periods of "retrenchment and readjustment": 1981 to 1982, 1986, and 1989 to 1990.[48] In each of these periods, administrative orders and mandatory schemes were hired to remedy the imbalances that resulted from excessive investment and consumption. The three waves of "retrenchment and readjustment" caused temporary recessions and shocks to the process of economic reform. Facing the center's efforts to tighten central control, localities and state-owned enterprises usually cooperated to protect their common interests. The central government repeatedly criticized local authorities for "not doing what is ordered but doing what is prohibited, using local strategies to counter the central policies, complying overtly but opposing covertly."[49] As the control of the central government was considerably weakened, the difficulty of mandatory retrenchment increased. From 1984 to 1989, the central government's budget revenue as a share of the total revenue of governments at all levels decreased from 56.1 percent to 39.1 percent. The central government only controlled 40 percent of the nation's foreign exchange revenue in 1989.[50]

The three waves of "retrenchment and readjustment" in the 1980s reflected fluctuation and wavering of government policies toward economic reform. This bred a rational expectation in the public for a changeable institutional environment. Responding to this expectation, localities and enterprises hastily drove to expand capital construction and consumption whenever the economic situation showed a relatively "warmer" phase of the central government's policy. Therefore, the problem of "hyper-investment," that each locality or administrative organ has a stake in developing as wide a range of industries and social facilities as possible, was not solved and became worse. To a large extent, the central government lost control over the money supply, increases in wages, and other monetary incomes. From 1984 to 1988, the national income increased 70 percent (at fixed prices), but capital investment increased 214 percent, household monetary income increased 200 percent.[51] China also experienced a significant increase in its foreign trade deficit because of the sharp increase in import purchases in 1985 and 1988 (Figure 7.9).

Both the low efficiency of state-owned enterprises and the excessive demand for investment and consumption funds were results of vertical rent-seeking by local bureaucrats and enterprise managers. The drain of state revenues greatly worsened the budget conditions of the central government. In the late 1980s, the state budget deficit increased sharply (Figure 7.10) and the state revenue as a percentage of national income declined sharply in the 1980s (Figure 7.11). As a Party document admitted, the growing internal debt and draining foreign exchange reserves in the late 1980s suggested serious budget difficulties.[52]

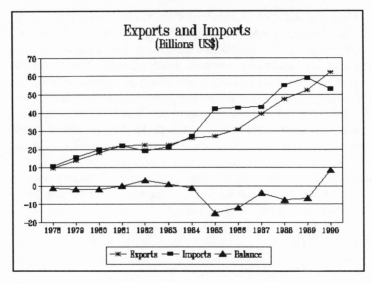

Figure 7.9

Source: *China Statistical Abstract* 1989, T 7.15; State Statistical Bureau's Statistical Communique on China's Economic and Social Development, 1989, 1990 *Renmin Ribao(People's Daily)*.

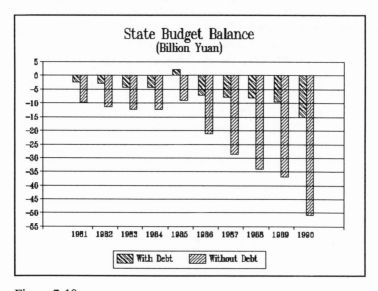

Figure 7.10

Source: *China Statistical Abstract* 1989; *Statistical Yearbook of China*, 1991.

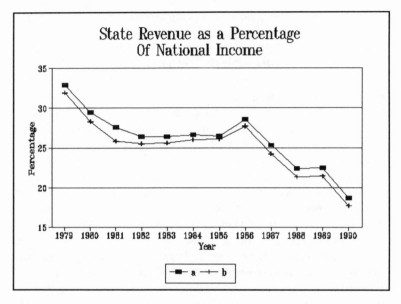

State Revenue as a Percentage
Of National Income

Figure 7.11
Source: *China Statistical Abstract 1989*, T 1.9; *Renmin Ribao (People's Daily)*'s related reports.
Legend: a--Including foreign borrowing; b--Excluding foreign borrowing

7.4 Corruption Everywhere

Rampant bureaucratic corruption and economic crimes featured the economic disorder of the 1980s. Bureaucratic corruption is a horizontal rent-seeking activity conducted by bureaucrats and entrepreneurs to obtain the contrived benefits associated with goods or services in shortage. According to Sanchez and Waters,[53] three conditions are necessary for the existence of bureaucratic corruption: (a) Contrived scarcity and its associated rent, which emerges whenever government intervention has created persistent disequilibria; (b) The transferability of property rights, which ensures that both the bureaucrats and prospective givers of bribes are allowed to possess transferable property rights; (c) The belief by each corrupt official that his own actions, as part of the bureaucratic structure, is not harmful to his personal wealth and well-being. In this perspective, the post-reform growth of economic crimes can be imputed to the following factors:

The introduction of the dual pricing system.
Disequilibria have existed extensively in the centrally-planned economy of China. One could pursue the rent associated with these disequilibria via arbitrage between planned prices and non-planned market prices. Even during the Mao era, the semi-legal and non-planned trade became a part of China's economic mechanism (see Chapter 5). In the early 1980s, the government partially legitimized the non-planned trade of raw materials, machinery, and products through the introduction of the dual pricing system. If this system had led to the abandonment of official pricing, the equilibrating entrepreneurship could be expected to generate a vector of equilibrium prices. But this did not happen. Under the dual pricing system, official pricing of some important goods was still maintained for planned supply quotas. The dual pricing was supposed to encourage supply of the goods in shortage by allowing producers to sell these goods at prices determined by demand and supply after they meet planned supply quotas. It was also intended to encourage enterprises receiving planned supply quotas to economize their inputs. Nevertheless, as soon as dual pricing was put into practice, it induced entrepreneurial activities aiming to seek the contrived benefits associated with planned quotas. For instance, bureaucrats in charge of rationing planned supply quotas now received bribes for providing quotas to non-planned customers. Enterprises producing the goods associated with planned quotas attempted to hide their real production and to sell their products directly on the market, ignoring their obligations to meet planned targets. Institutions receiving planned supply quotas sought to resell the planned quota for higher profits. A Party document acknowledged: "The dual pricing system of the means of production has become a hotbed of economic disorder and corruption."[54] The availability of contrived benefits under the dual pricing system satisfies the first of the Sanchez-Waters conditions.

The development of private ownership.
Possession of transferable property right became feasible and accumulation of personal wealth was greatly facilitated as the private economy revived and the general freedom in daily economic life increased in the 1980s.[55] Personal possession and accumulation of wealth were no longer a taboo as was in the Mao era. Stock exchanges, hard currency swatch centers, and real estate markets all emerged in the late 1980s. A scramble for riches broke out as the new "money elite" became part of the upper-class in society.[56] The development of

private ownership therefore provided an important basis for the growth of bureaucratic corruption, the second of the conditions set up by Sanchez and Waters.

The weakening of ideological control.
The conflicts between market-oriented reform and orthodox Marxism shook the ideological basis of the communist system. This factor, although non-economic, constituted the third Sanchez-Waters condition for the growth of bureaucratic corruption. The bureaucracy became more vulnerable to corruption as its members put money before ideology. Even higher ranking officials were not excepted. In 1989, for instance, the number of officials above county level who involved in corruption cases was 875, 3.5 times more than the previous year. This number reached 790 in the first six months of 1990.[57]

Besides these factors associated with the Sanchez-Waters conditions, economic reforms of the 1980s resulted in some other factors that might have contributed to the increase of corruption. These include an unstable legal framework, a social cynicism toward law and order, and the weak enforcement of law. These factors came from the fact that these reforms were a continuous process of destroying the established institutions of a centrally-planned economy. As shown in Chapter 6 many aspects of the reforms were not introduced and pre-designed by the government. A series of institutional innovations initiated by private entrepreneurs featured these reforms. Most reforms concerning the private sector, for instance, were achieved through the interaction between official concessions and private entrepreneurs' actions to defy the existing orders and to try the margins of official tolerance. This process was by no means smooth and costless.

The legal framework in transition.
The legal framework inherited from the Mao era was mainly built according to the principles of traditional central planning. When the economy embarked on the path of market-oriented reform in the 1980s, the legal system appeared as a straight-jacket for reformers. A widespread saying in China in the mid 1980s expressed the frustration: "What looks reasonable may be illegal but what is legal looks really unreasonable." While the economic reforms continued, the legal system also underwent a transition to accommodate itself to rapid institutional changes in the economic structure. The rebuilding of the legal system

was a slow and tedious job. Beginning in 1983, the State Council began to carry out a nationwide clearing of old regulations, provisions, and bylaws to update the whole legal system.[58] Nonetheless, most of the do's and do-not's were not defined by the laws, but by the Party's or State Council's documents. The legitimate scope of activity of production and trade by peasants was not defined by legislation but by the Central Committee of the Party in its "Number One Document" issued each January in the 1980s.[59] The government also issued circulars labeled with "Temporary Regulations" or "Temporary Provisions" to determine the legitimate scope of economic activities. For instance, in 1985, the State Council issued three such documents to tighten controls on retail prices.[60] From 1979 to 1987, China's legislative organs, the People's Congress and its Standing Committee, formulated 58 laws and adopted 56 resolutions amending or supplementing laws and other decisions regarding legislation (of which 50 percent were economic laws). In comparison, there were 500 administrative regulations and provisions stipulated by the central government, 949 by the provincial governments.[61] The extensive and changeable administrative interventions in economic life made the legal system unstable and confusing. Besides, the policy of *shidian*[62] resulted in the heterogeneous development of economic reforms between different regions. This created further confusion in the identification of illegal activities, because what had become legitimate in some experimental provinces or cities might still remain illegal in other areas. A well-known case of speculative trade was the "illegal trade of cars in Island Hainan." The local government of Island Hainan was authorized to practice more radical reforms and import privilege of production equipment in the mid-1980s. Later, however, the Hainan locality was accused of abusing the privilege to profiteer by importing cars and reselling them to other provinces.[63] Since the legal system was in a status of uncertainly, both bureaucrats in charge of economic affairs and business managers became more likely to commit economic crimes in the 1980s.

The social cynicism toward law and order.

The instability of the legal framework cultivated a social cynicism toward law and order in China. In the process of economic reform, the acting of private entrepreneurs repeatedly violated official restrictions and resulted in institutional innovations. A negative side effect of this process was that people lost respect for existing laws. Even the government looked to legislation as a tool to implement the Party's policies. Legislative changes were usually made to meet the changes of the Party's guidelines. The State Council's "Decision on Clearing the Regulations and By-laws" in 1983, for instance, asserted that the legislative changes should be made according to the current guidelines and policies of the Party.[64] At the end of 1989, the Party announced a ban on private firms' operation of long-distance transportation for wholesale purposes and trading the means of production,[65] regardless of the fact that these activities had been legitimized by a regulation issued by the state council in 1983 and a bylaw passed by the People's Congress in 1988.[66] In practice, the Party and government's mandatory controls were more authoritative than the existing laws. Generally, it was the Party, the government, and even individual officials who decided the definition of legal and illegal activities.

The uncertainty of policy changes and the cynicism toward law encouraged myopic behavior and illegal activity by private entrepreneurs. A variety of surveys in the 1980s showed that most private entrepreneurs viewed their jobs as temporary.[67] According to a government report, a considerable number of private enterprises did not have a standard accounting system, had no intention of long-run investment, and engaged in illegal business activities by using fake trademarks and even selling phony products.[68] Tax evasion was popular among private enterprises as the government imposed higher tax rates on the private sector. Tax collection officials in Shanghai estimated in 1989 that about 70 percent of individual laborers (private business owners) committed tax evasion.[69] Before 1988, the private business income tax rate was 60 to 84 percent.[70] The 1988 regulation on private business income tax reduced the business income tax rate to 35 percent, but imposed a 40 percent adjustment tax on the personal income of business owners.[71] In 1989, a new tax, the circulation tax, was added, and seven percent of after-tax profits were levied to fund "construction of power and transportation networks."[72]

The weak enforcement of law.
The enforcement of laws was generally weak in the 1980s. As a government report admitted, the practice of ignoring existing laws and the weak enforcement of laws "still widely exist[ed]."[73] In China, the judicial and procuratorial organs are not independent of the Party leadership and the administration. The judges, procurators, and other members of law enforcement staff are part of the bureaucratic hierarchy

and follow the instructions of the Party committees at corresponding levels. The introduction of the contract responsibility system and the government revenue sharing system in the 1980s created conditions of collaboration between the local governments and enterprises. Therefore, many localities turned a blind eye to the illegal operations of subordinate enterprises as long as these activities would increase local revenues without causing too much trouble. In many cases, local governments played the role of protector of illegal traders.[74] In his annual report to the People's Congress, Ren Jianxin, the head of the Highest Court, warned that "local protectionism" had seriously interfered in the enforcement of law.[75] Meanwhile, many administrative organs of the Party and the government were also involved in illegal trade of goods that were in their charge. An editorial of *Renmin Ribao (People's Daily)* pointed out that "*guan dao*" (bureaucratic involvement in illegal trade) committed by official organs had become a serious problem.[76] A major difficulty of the campaign against corruption was the involvement of a number of high ranking officials and their family members in "*guan dao*" and other economic crimes.[77]

These institutional characteristics of China's law enforcement system resulted in the low risk for committing economic crimes. For instance, in mid-1988, the number of so-called "briefcase corporations," that is, corporations doing speculative business without real capital or productive facilities, reached 40,000. Most of these corporations were run by the Party and administrative organs. Among them more than 700 were run by the ministries at the central level.[78] In 1988 and 1989, however, although the central government started a campaign against corruption, only about 1,000 officials above county level were investigated or prosecuted for corruption cases.[79] It appears that government officials were less likely to be punished than ordinary citizens when they are involved in economic crimes. For example, in 1990, of the accepted cases regarding tax evasion, which involved mostly common citizens, about 62 percent cases were filed and prosecuted. Of the accepted cases regarding corruption, which generally involved officials, less than 50 percent were filed and prosecuted. The latter ratio was consistently lower than the former ratio for other years, too. It was also consistently lower than the prosecution ratio of all accepted cases of economic crimes.[80] Ren Jianxin complained in his report that many cases of economic crimes were not prosecuted because the practice of "*yi fa dai xing*" (using monetary fines to replace legal punishment) by the administrative organs.[81] The low risk of committing economic crimes constituted a major reason of rampant growth of bureaucratic corruption in the 1980s.

7.5 Concluding Comments

The political-social tensions in the late 1980s were closely related to the chaotic economic situation. The previous discussion shows that China's economic reform of the 1980s was infected with serious institutional defects. The transitional economic system provided numerous opportunities for entrepreneurial rent seeking and, therefore, depleted the vigor of economic growth. In fact, in addition to the runaway inflation, socioeconomic disorders, and worsening disparity of incomes, China's economy in the late 1980s also suffered a slowdown of economic growth. It failed to sustain the momentum of economic growth that it had enjoyed in the early stages of the reform. From 1978 to 1988, real per capita national income increased from 315 yuan to 613.86 yuan (in 1978's value), increasing 94.9 percent, with an average annual growth rate of 6.9 percent. During the last three years of the 1980s, however, the growth slowed down (Figure 7.12).

The facts presented in the chapter support some important theoretical results obtained in earlier chapters. The relationship between entrepreneurial activities and the chaotic aspects of economic reform confirms that the welfare effects of entrepreneurship are highly sensitive to the institutional environment. In the 1980s institutional changes generated new opportunities for vertical rent seeking in the state-owned sector. Rent-seeking competition among enterprises led to the unproductive use of the entrepreneurial resources of managers. As a result, economic reform failed to improve the efficiency of state-owned enterprises. The low efficiency of state-owned enterprises and the drain of state revenues led to serious macroeconomic difficulties in the late 1980s. Meanwhile, market distortions and a transitional legal framework encouraged horizontal rent seeking in the form of economic crimes, especially the crimes of embezzlement and bribery. The resulting bureaucratic corruption and economic disorders increased social tensions in the transitional Chinese economy. Campaigns against economic crimes were also costly for society. Therefore, both vertical and horizontal rent-seeking activities, although entrepreneurial in nature, caused considerable social welfare losses.

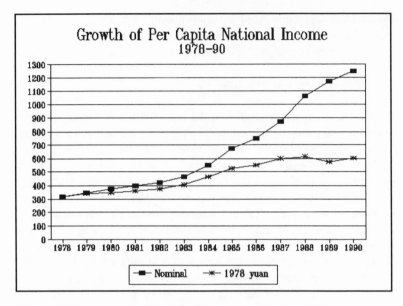

Figure 7.12
Source: *China Trade and Price Statistics* 1988; *China Statistical Abstract* 1989; *Renmin Ribao (People's Daily)*, 22 Feb. 1990, p. 3, 23 Feb. 1991, p. 3.

In the economic reform of the 1980s, decision-making power was decentralized to lower levels of the planning hierarchy, especially to localities. Under the contract responsibility system and the revenue-sharing system, the local government and enterprises shared more common interests in retaining revenue for local development. Therefore, state-owned enterprises and local governments developed a closer working relationship between each other. The vertical rent-seeking acting of enterprises was more effective than before. The increased fortune of vertical rent seeking reduced managers' interest in productivity improvement. This contributed to the declining efficiency in the state sector.

    The growth of bureaucratic corruption was a direct result of more effective horizontal rent-seeking and the increasing number of rent-seekers. The effectiveness of horizontal rent seeking was enhanced by the introduction of the dual pricing system, and the low risk of illegal activities that resulted from social cynicism. The transitional legal system and the weak enforcement of law further encouraged the activity.

The previous analysis suggests some important policy implications: The source of vertical rent seeking among local authorities and state-owned enterprises was their opportunities to manipulate taxation and use non-market methods to allocate financial resources. If the financial independence of these enterprises had been provided by better defined property right and uniform taxation, their efficiency could have improved. Meanwhile, if the allocation of financial resources had not been determined through bureaucratic procedures but by market demand and supply, the vertical rent seeking for these resources could have been eliminated. Finally, the manipulation of the tax rate and real income of enterprises because of "objective conditions" would have been unlikely had free markets been allowed to generate the correct price signals.

The foremost condition for horizontal rent seeking is contrived scarcity, which results from market distortions and price controls. Therefore, the establishment of a well-ordered free market economy could have eliminated a great number of horizontal rent-seeking opportunities in China. In addition, if the economic reform had followed a more systematic strategy and minimized the necessity for private entrepreneurs to start institutional innovation, the evolution of the institutional framework could have occurred more smoothly through legal procedures. We would then have found the problem of social cynicism toward law and order less serious. Also, a legislative and judicial system independent of the Party's influence and administrative intervention would have been a more effective and authoritative alternative. An efficient law enforcement system is vital to the development of property rights and market order.

NOTES

1. Jefferies, Ian, *A Guide to the Socialist Economies*, London and New York: Routledge, 1990, p. 239.

2. *Renmin Ribao (People's Daily)*, 17 Aug. 1988, p. 1.

3. A national survey showed that by the spring of 1989, 78.15 percent of the population rated "bureaucratic corruption" as their most pressing social problem. [*Zhongguo Zhi Chun (China Spring)*, no. 81, Feb 1990, p. 37]

4. Xie Baogui, "The Function of the Chinese Procuratorial Organ in the Combat against Corruption," *Asian Journal of Public Administration*, Vol. 10, no. 1, Jun 1988, pp. 73-75.

5. *P. R. China Yearbook*, Beijing, China: Yearbook Press, 1981, p. 304, 1983 p. 472; *Renmin Ribao (People's Daily)*, 16 March 1990, p. 3, 13 April 1991, p. 4.

6. *P. R. China Yearbook*, 1981, p. 307.

7. *P. R. China Yearbook*, 1987, p. 164.

8. *P.R. China Yearbook*, 1987, p. 164.

9. *Renmin Ribao (People's Daily)*, 7 July 1990, p. 1.

10. Hua Sheng, "Corruption: The Cancer of the CPC," *Tansuo (Quest)* [Hong Kong], no. 4 1990 (76), pp. 59-61.

11. Zhang, Renze and Mo-yin S. Tam, "Changes in Income Distributions in China in the Process of Economic Reform in the 1980s: a Welfare Approach," Working paper, University of Illinois at Chicago, 1990.

12. State Statistical Bureau's annual Communique on China' Economic and Social Development, 1987 to 1989, *Renmin Ribao (People's Daily)*, 25 Feb. 1988, p. 3; 2 March 1989, p. 3; 22 Feb. 1990, p. 3. No

corresponding figures available for other years in the 1980s.

13. Jiang Zemin, "Speech on the Fortieth Anniversary of the Founding of the P.R.C.," *Renmin Ribao (People's Daily)*, 30 Sept. 1989, p. 2.

14. *Zhongguo Tongji Nianjian* (Statistical Yearbook of China) 1991, T 4.34, p. 130.

15. Ibid., T 8.9, p. 93.

16. *Renmin Ribao (People's Daily)*, 29 May 1990, p. 3, and the figures are calculated with reference to "the State Bureau of Statistics' Communique on China's Economic and Social Development of 1989," *Renmin Ribao (People's Daily)*, 22 Feb. 1990, p. 3.

17. See *China Urban Statistics 1988*, New York: Praeger, 1989, xi-xiv.

18. These ratios are calculated according to *China Urban Statistics 1988*, T 15, T 57, and T 59.

19. Jefferies, op. cit., p. 220.

20. *Renmin Ribao (People's Daily)*, 18 Aug. 1988, p. 1.

21. *Renmin Ribao (People's Daily)*, 19 Aug. 1988, p. 1, 24 Aug. 1988, p. 1.

22.*Renmin Ribao (People's Daily)*, 18 Aug. 1988, p. 1.

23. *Renmin Ribao (People's Daily)*, 18 Aug. 1988, p. 1.

24. *Almanac of China's Economy 1989*, p. II:6.

25. *Renmin Ribao (People's Daily)*, 28 Oct. 1988, p. 1.

26. *Renmin Ribao (People's Daily)*, 22 Jan. 1989, p. 1.

27. The Central Committee of the CPC, "The Resolution on Further Retrenchment and Deepening of Economic Reform," *Renmin Ribao (People's Daily)*, 17 Jan. 1990, p. 1.

28. The Chinese government started to issue government bonds at home and abroad in the early 1980s. As domestic financial markets developed, government borrowing became more and more important in financing the budget deficit.

29. Janos Kornai, "The Hungarian Reform Process: Vision, Hopes, and Reality," *Journal of Economic Literature*, Vol 24, Dec. 1986, pp. 1687-1737; *Contradictions and Dilemmas,* Cambridge: First MIT Press edition, 1986; also see H.S. Levine, "On the Nature and Location of Entrepreneurial Activity in Centrally Planned Economies: The Soviet Case," in *Entrepreneurship,* Joshua Ronen ed., Lexington, MA: Lexington Books, pp. 235-267, for the institutional inconsistencies between the centrally-planned system and innovative entrepreneurship.

30. Kornai, Ibid.

31. The Central Committee of the CPC, "Resolution on Restructuring Economic System," *Renmin Ribao (People's Daily)*, 22 Oct. 1984.

32. See *Decision of the Central Committee of the CPC on Reform of the Economic Structure,* in the appendix of Liu and Wu ed. op. cit.

33. Hua Sheng et al., "Ten Year in China's Reform: Looking back, reflection, and prospect," *Jingji Yanjiu (Economic Research)*, no. 9, Sept. 1988, pp. 13-37; Shi Xiaomin and Liu Jirui, "Review on 'Ten Years in China's Reform'," *Jingji Yanjiu (Economic Research)*, no. 2, 1989, pp. 11-33.

34. In Guangdong Province, for example, a typically contracted enterprise would be bounded to increase its submission to the government on a seven percent annual rate in three years on the base of its profits and taxes submitted in the contracted year; of the profits surpassing the contracted submission, eighty to ninety percent would go to the enterprise, and ten to twenty percent to the government. [*Jiefang Ribao (Liberation Daily)* [Shanghai, China], 4 Feb. 1988, p. 2.]

35. Zhao Ziyang, "The Report on the Third Plenary of the 13th Central Committee of the CPC," *Renmin Ribao (People's Daily)*, 28 October 1988.

36. *Shijie Jingji Daobao (The World Economic Herald)* [Shanghai, China], 19 Dec. 1988, p. 15.

37. Wu Jinglian and Bruce Reynolds, "Choosing a Strategy for China's Economic Reform," paper presented at the annual meetings of the American Economic Association, Chicago, December 1987.

38. See Walder, Andrew G., "Local Bargaining Relationships and Urban Industrial Finance," in *Bureaucracy, Politics, and Decision Making in Post-Mao China*, K. Lieberthal and D. Lampton ed., Berkeley, California: University of California Press, 1992, for a more detailed description of the bargaining relationships concerning the effective tax rates and financial support.

39. Walder, op. cit. pp. 16-19.

40. Blejer, M. I. and G. Szapary, "The Changing Role of Macro-economic Policies in China," *Financial Development*, Vol. 27, no. 2, 1990, pp. 32-35.

41. Walder, op. cit.

42. There were other elements that contributed to the low efficiency of state-owned enterprises. For instance, the existence of the private economy and its related high personal income made the improvement of incentive schemes within the state-owned sector less effective.

43. *Renmin Ribao (People's Daily)*, 6 April 1990, p. 2.

44. Estimated according to my recalculation based on *China Statistical Abstract* 1989, T 4.1, T 7.3, and T 7.7.

45. *Renmin Ribao (People's Daily)*, 8 April 1989, p. 4.

46. Blejer and Szapary, op. cit., p. 33.

47. For instance, in the retrenchment of the period 1988 to 1989, the State Council ordered that all capital investment projects belonging to nine categories should be shut down without exception even before they received government inspection [*Renmin Ribao (People's Daily)*, 7 Jan.

1989, p. 3]. Also, see *Renmin Ribao (People's Daily)*, 14 Oct. 1988, p. 1 for more administrative methods adopted in the retrenchment.

48. Harding, op. cit., pp. 71-73; *Renmin Ribao (People's Daily)*, 28 Oct. 1988, p. 1, and 17 Jan. 1990, p. 1.

49. The Central Committee of the CPC, "Resolution on Further Economic Retrenchment," *Renmin Ribao (People's Daily)*, 17 Jan. 1990, p. 4.

50. *Renmin Ribao (People's Daily)*, 17 Jan. 1990, p. 1, 10 April 1990, p. 3.

51. The Central Committee of the CPC, "The Resolution on Further Economic Retrenchment," *Renmin Ribao (People's Daily)*, 17 Jan 1990, p. 1.

52. Ibid., p. 1.

53. Sanchez, N. and A. R. Waters, "Controlling Corruption in Africa and Latin America," in *The Economics of Property Rights*, E. G. Furuboton and S. Pejovich ed., Cambridge, Mass.: Ballinger Publishing Company, 1974, pp. 279-295.

54. The Central Committee of the CPC, "The Resolution on Further Retrenchment," *Renmin Ribao (People's Daily)*, 17 Jan. 1990, p. 4.

55. See Chapter 6 for a more detailed account of the revival of the private economy in the 1980s.

56. Kraus, Willy, *Private Business in China,* Honolulu, Hawaii: University of Hawaii Press, 1991, pp.180-184.

57. *Renmin Ribao (People's Daily)*, 16 March 1990, p. 3; 9 Aug. 1990, p. 4.

58. *Almanac of China's Economy 1984*, p. IV:70.

59. *Yearbook on Chinese Communism 1989*, p. IV:37-8.

60. *Almanac of China's Economy* 1986, p. V:50.

61. *China Facts & Figures Annual* (1988), p. 301.

62. See the explanation of the policy of *Shidian* in Section 7.1.

63. *Almanac of China's Economy 1984*, p. IV:70. *Yearbook on Chinese Communism 1989*, p. VI:81.

64. *Almanac of China's Economy* 1984, p. IV:70. *Yearbook on Chinese Communism* 1989, p. VI:81.

65. The Central Committee of the CPC, "The Resolution on Further Retrenchment," *Renmin Ribao (People's Daily)*, 17 Jan. 1990, p. 4.

66. The State Council, "Some Supplementary Regulations on the Urban Non-agricultural Individual Economy," *Almanac of China's Economy* 1984, p. IX:55; "The PRC Temporary Bylaw of the Private Enterprises," *Renmin Ribao (People's Daily)*, 30 June 1988, p. 3.

67. Rosen, S. "The Private Economy," *Chinese Economic Studies*, Vol. 21, no.1, 1987, p. 4.

68. *Renmin Ribao (People's Daily)*, 11 May 1989, p. 3.

69. China News Agency, 10 Jan. 1989.

70. *Almanac of China's Economy 1988*, p. XI:158.

71. "The PRC Temporary Bylaws on Private Enterprises' Business Income Tax," and the State Council's "Regulation of Personal Income Adjustment Tax on Private Business Investors," *Renmin Ribao (People's Daily)* 30 June 1988, p. 3.

72. *Shijie Ribao (The World Daily)* [New York, US], 26 Oct. 1989, p. 32.

73. Li Peng, "The Report to the Third Meeting of the Seventh National People's Congress," *Renmin Ribao (People's Daily)*, 6 April 1990, p. 4.

74. *Yearbook on Chinese Communism* 1989, p. VI:81.

75. *Renmin Ribao (People's Daily)*, 13 April 1991, p. 3.

76. *Renmin Ribao (People's Daily)*, 14 July 1988, p. 1.

77. *Yearbook on Chinese Communism 1989*, p. VI:83.

78. *Gongren Ribao (Workers' Daily)*, 24 Aug. 1988.

79. Estimated according to the report on *Renmin Ribao (People's Daily)*, 16 March 1990, p. 3.

80. *Zhongguo Jiancha Nianjian (Procuratorial Yearbook of China)*, Beijing: China Procuratorial Press, 1991.

81. *Renmin Ribao (People's Daily)*, 13 April 1991, p. 3.

CHAPTER 8

EPILOGUE: PROSPECTS FOR THE FUTURE

8.1 Introduction

The private-sector experience in China shows that the waxing and waning of China's private sector have been closely related to changes of its institutional environment. Lack of entrepreneurial spirit never seems to be a problem for Chinese society. Even during the Mao era, whenever the official suppression of market transaction relaxed a bit, the number of people engaged in the private sector immediately bounced back. The underground economy never ceased to operate even in the most suppressive years. The review of China's private-sector experience confirms that what really matter are the institutional settings that allocate entrepreneurial resources among different uses.

What does this review imply for the future development of entrepreneurship in China? Will the private-sector boom continue in the post-Deng era? What will be the features of Chinese entrepreneurship in the coming years? This chapter will examine the factors that may affect the institutional settings of China's private sector in the foreseeable future.

Section 8.2 explains why the setback of reforms by the end of the 1980s was so short-lived. Several factors that helped ending the setback are identified. Section 8.3 examines the government's pragmatic considerations as the basis of the recent surge of market-oriented reforms and the continuing liberal policies toward the private and other non-state sectors in the 1990s. The last section speculates on the prospects of China's private entrepreneurship in the years after Deng.

171

8.2 A Short-lived Setback of Reforms

Since China entered the 1990s, her economy has shocked the rest of the world with a double-digit economic growth in 1992 and 1993. Meanwhile, the country has accumulated remarkable economic achievements over a decade-long nine percent annual growth of her GNP.[1] By 1994, China's economy should be almost four times bigger than it was in 1978, the year when the economic reform started. If the momentum continues, China will be the biggest economy on earth in the next twenty years.[2] This looks highly likely. By a recent study of International Monetary Fund, China's economic size, if measured by purchasing power parity rather than exchange rates, was already the third largest behind the United States and Japan in 1992.[3] According to a study by Dwight Perkins, China in 1991 was in most ways a bit more advanced than South Korea was in 1970, a year when Korea's per capita GNP (in 1991 dollars) was $1,100.[4]

China's market-oriented reform also has entered a new stage. Since China's patriarch leader Deng Xiaoping urged the Party to speed up reform and opening to the world in early 1992, there has been a new surge of reforms toward a full-fledged open market economy. The Fourteenth National Congress of CPC (October 1992) established for the first time in the Party's official guideline the "socialist market economic system" as the goal of the reform.[5] This was an ideological "leap forward" from the somewhat ambiguous goal of the "socialist planned commodity economy" defined in the previous national congress of 1987. In November 1993, the Third Plenary of the Fourteenth CPC Central Committee passed a 50-article "decision" on the strategies of further reforms.[6] The Party leaders announced that "establishing a socialist market economic system means making the market a fundamental factor in the disposition of resources under state macro control."[7] The "decision" covers ten broad sectors dealing with the need to restructure the market system, state enterprises, government functions, taxation and social security, foreign trade and law. This document is a milestone of the Chinese leaders' efforts of "groping for planned stones" to restructure the economy.[8] These recent changes contrast sharply with what happened in the months after 1989 Tiananmen Event.

By the end of the 1980s, only about three years before the Fourteenth Congress, economic reforms in many fields came to a halt.

The non-state sectors experienced their most difficult period after the beginning of economic reform in 1978. As part of the economic retrenchment program, the government shut down more than a million rural enterprises and forced the demise of 2.2 million individual businesses.[9] As a result, in 1989, the number of individual businesses declined by 14.44 percent, and the number of their employees fell by 16.44 percent.[10] In the same year, the number of registered "private enterprises" fell from 90,600 to 76,600.[11] Meanwhile, rural township and village enterprises encountered unprecedented difficulties in form of shortage of funds, energy supply, and raw materials.[12] During the period from 1984 to 1988, the average annual growth rate of the total output value of rural township and village enterprises was around 30 to 40 percent; but it slid down significantly in 1989.[13] Besides the suppression of the private sector and rural industries, the government also reemphasized the importance of the collective economy in rural areas and sent signals of enforcing more strict central plans on agricultural production. For instance, the government decided in 1990 to "reassign contract land to households . . . and organize production under unified plans."[14] In the middle of 1991, the government announced the start of a new campaign of "Socialist Education" in rural areas to urge peasants to "insist on socialist direction," to "criticize ideology of private ownership," and to "revive collectivism." The main targets of the campaign were Party members, rural cadres, and private business owners. The ideological guidelines of this campaign sounded similar to that of the "Socialist Education" in 1964, which led to the disastrous Cultural Revolution.[15]

These changes reflected the temporary setback of the market-oriented reform after the Tiananmen Event.[16] Why was this setback so short-lived? The following factors reflect the difficulties for switching the economy back toward a centrally-planned system during the setback.

The first was the rise of the localism in China's economy. The contractual budget sharing system developed in the 1980s substantially decentralized the economic decision making in the administrative hierarchy. With the greater autonomy they gained, local governments have accumulated solid financial powers. The three experimental provinces for economic reform, Guangdong, Fujian, and Hainan, for instance, shared one third of the nation's total export in 1989.[17] With the development of local and rural industries, the fiscal revenue at the county level grew rapidly in the 1980s and accounted for over one fourth of the state budget in 1990. In 1990, there were 95 counties with fiscal revenue over 100 million yuan. Among them, ten counties had their fiscal revenue over 300 million yuan, approximately equal to the median provincial budget size.[18] The provincial governments captured up to 80 percent of the state budget revenues in the early 1990s.[19] Upon this basis of economic strength, some local governments have been able to develop their own economic policies that are different from those issued by the central government, especially those policies regulating the non-state sectors. It was reported that in 1989 and 1990 the leaders of Guangdong Province, backed by the financial support of business tycoons in Hong Kong, resisted the pressure from Beijing to implement the austerity program.[20] Many localities resisted the central government's efforts to unify the allocation of raw materials.[21] In 1989 and 1990, to attract foreign investment, especially the capital from Taiwan and Hong Kong, a number of provinces and localities promulgated their own favorable policies. These locally initiated policies emerged in such a scale that the Party's Central Committee finally took steps to intervene. The Central Committee urged the administration to "strictly implement unified state regulations and policies to encourage foreign investment" and "stop the competitive promulgation of favorable measures [to attract foreign investment]."[22] During the retrenchment period started in 1989, many local governments continued to encourage the development of rural industries and private businesses. The governments of some provinces, such as Jiangsu, Zhejiang, Shanghai, Fujian, and Shandong, authorized rural township and village enterprises to do foreign trade and develop joint ventures with foreign businesses. The Guangdong provincial government even encouraged private enterprises to develop business abroad. In this way, they helped the non-state sectors to survive the most difficult period of the retrenchment program. Consequently, the private businesses and rural industries in these provinces led the recovery of the national economy in the first half of 1990.[23]

The second factor was the maturity of private entrepreneurship itself. After a decade of growth, most of the private enterprises had learned to survive political changes and had successfully improved their business environment by pushing for institutional reforms. As shown in earlier chapters, in those areas where non-state sectors had prospered, private entrepreneurs and local bureaucrats developed close cooperation and common interests. In addition, the policies tolerating private businesses were formalized by law in the late 1980s. The legal right of private businesspeople was, at least on paper, protected against discretionary policy changes.[24] Managers and owners of the non-state enterprises had also accumulated managerial experience and improved the quality of their labor force. The number of professional technicians employed by rural industries increased fifty times from 1983 to 1989. During the period 1986 to 1990, the percentage of employees who had received education beyond primary school level increased from 30 percent to 64.8 percent.[25]

There was, perhaps, the third factor that made the effective implementation of any setback from market-oriented reform difficult: the widespread bureaucratic corruption among government staff. Although the government tried to reclaim the loyalty of its staff by reenforcing ideological education, there was little sign that such attempts were successful.

By the end of 1990, a strong recovery of the private sector occurred. In 1990 the number of individual businesses increased by 6.5 percent and their registered capital increased by 14.3 percent. In the same year the number of private enterprises increased by 8.3 percent and their registered capital increased by 12.6 percent.[26] The miraculous recovery of private businesses and the rapid growth of the rural industries in 1990 exhibited the vigor of the non-state sectors and exposed the government's impotence in carrying out hardline policies toward the non-state sectors.

The quick end of the reform-setback was also part of the policy adjustment made by the central government. Apparently, pragmatic considerations have overtaken ideology in the first few years of the 1990s as it did in most of the 1980s.

8.3 Pragmatic Considerations of the 1990s

Throughout the period from the 1950s to the 1980s, the institutional environment of the private sector was drastically affected by the wavering of the political pendulum. The source of the instability of official policies was the conflicts between the communist ideology and the pragmatic political considerations. On the one hand, the Marxist-Maoist ideology defines central planning, public ownership and egalitarian income distribution as principles for a socialist society. On the other hand, the reality that China was an underdeveloped economy with the world's largest population forced the political leaders to look for pragmatic policies to solve the emergent economic problems they faced. The conflicts between the ideological guideline and pragmatic considerations were the characteristics of economic policy making in China. The 1980s' reform was a result of the overwhelming pragmatism in official policy making.

As shown earlier, the relatively liberal policies toward the private and other non-state sectors in the 1980s were adopted mainly as pragmatic measures to ease some immediate economic pressures. These pressures included the problem of unemployment, inadequate supply of service and retail industries, and the need to finance government revenues. The liberal policies helped China successfully cope with these problems in the 1980s. Nonetheless, similar worries are still pending upon government decision makers in the 1990s.

a. The pressure of unemployment. From 1980 to 1992, the Chinese economy created 51 million non-agricultural jobs. Of these jobs, about 44 percent were generated by the non-state sectors.[27] According to Ruan Congwu, the (former) Minister of China's Labor Department, the first half of the 1990s would see a peak of employment pressure because of the baby boom in the 1970s. In each of the first five years of the 1990s there would be 11 million people entering the labor market. He promised that the government would do everything it could to keep the [urban] unemployment rate under 3.5 percent, compared with the current rate 2.6 percent. The state sector, however, would only be able to absorb about seven million new employees every year. The government would therefore encourage the rest of the job seekers to create self-employment opportunities.[28]

Another source of unemployment pressure comes from the surplus labor in rural areas. As pointed out by some Chinese economists, if the rural surplus labor force was counted, the real number of currently unemployed people could be close to 30 million, ten times higher than the official statistics.[29] A phenomenal event in the recent years has been the massive flow of thousands of rural job-seekers into the big cities. This floating population has caused a series of socioeconomic problems.[30] Under these pressures, the only way for the government to keep unemployment rate low enough to avoid social unrest is to maintain a policy of encouragement toward the non-state sectors. For example, during the period of the Seventh Five-year Plan (1986 to 1990), the rural township and village enterprises created 22 million job opportunities, accounting for 57.6 percent of the total increase in jobs.

Nearly 100 million or 20 percent of the rural labor force was employed by these enterprises.[31]

b. The need to sustain economic growth. Although China's GNP has grown by an average of almost nine percent a year since the economic reform started in 1978, economic growth is still a challenging issue to the Chinese leaders. This is because the base of this high growth rate is a generally underdeveloped economy with a level of per capita income in 1992 merely equals to US$ 380, although this figure is suspiciously low.[32] Besides, China has the world's largest population to feed. A considerable increase of GNP would be much less impressive when it is divided by the number 1.2 billion —— the number of people dwelling in the country. That partially explains why the growth of per capita national income slowed for the country in the late 1980s (See Figure 7.12). In the second half of the 1980s, China's population grew at an annual rate of 1.55 percent. On the base of the population in 1990, this means an annual increase of 17.7 million people.[33] The government is aware that if China cannot sustain a high growth rate she has achieved so far, the stagnant of living standards will jeopardize the social-political stability.[34]

Table 8.1 Annual Growth Rate of Gross Output Value of Industry

Year	Total	State	Collective (Total)	Township & Village	Individual	Foreign
1986	11.1	6.2	16.7	37.9	60.6	73.7
1987	16.5	11.0	25.0	33.9	48.0	98.0
1988	20.7	12.7	28.8	35.0	46.0	97.0
1989	8.3	3.7	10.7	12.7	24.1	44.7
1990	7.6	2.9	9.1	12.5	21.6	56.6
Average	13.1	7.3	17.6	25.9	39.2	74.0

Note: the growth rates were calculated on comparable prices. The "Foreign" category includes businesses owned by foreigners, overseas Chinese, and businesspeople from Hong Kong, Macao and Taiwan; it also includes joint-ventures.

Source: The State Statistic Bureau's Annual Statistical Communique on China's Economic and Social Development, 1986 to 1990. The State Statistic Bureau's Report on Accomplishment of the Seventh Five-Year Plan, *People's Daily*, 14 March 1991.

The non-state sectors, by any measure, have been the engines of growth. After a decade of economic reform, the private and rural businesses have not only become an important part of the national economy, but also constituted its most dynamic component. For instance, the outstanding performance of these enterprises increased their share of gross industrial product value to one third and helped to raise China's industrial growth rate to seven percent in 1990.[35]

c. The fiscal revenue problem. The non-state sectors became a major source of the government fiscal revenue in the 1980s. From 1986 to 1990, taxes collected from rural township and village enterprises totaled 190 billion yuan, with an average of 38 billion yuan per year. These enterprises contributed about half of the net increase of state revenue in this period. In addition, the government collected taxes worth several billion yuan each year from the private sector.[36] A sharply contrasting fact is: In the late 1980s the government paid forty to sixty billion yuan each year to subsidize state-owned enterprises. The existence of the non-state sectors has therefore been vital to the state budget.[37] Meanwhile, the problem of relatively slow growth of the state sector remains unsolved. The state-owned enterprises experienced great difficulties in improving their efficiency in the 1980s (See Figure 7.8). Entering the 1990s, the chance for the government to improve the efficiency of the state sector does not look much better. Comparing 1990 with 1988, the profits and tax revenues earned by the state-owned enterprises dropped by 15.3 percent. The percentage of these enterprises that are losing money climbed from 10.9 percent to 27.6 percent, and the total loss increased by 3.3 times.[38] By October 1993, 33.8 percent of state firms went into the red, with losses amounting to 27 billion yuan.[39]

With the above pressures in place, it will be highly irrational for any political leader in the future to reverse the government's tolerant policy toward non-state sectors. However, the Party's ideology and the seemingly endless power struggle within the leadership have always influenced China's economic policy making in the past decades. Even during the reform decade of the 1980s, two general secretaries of the Party were ejected in power struggles. The Chinese leaders' slow and painful approach toward a market-oriented reform goal in the 1980s reflected the conflict between their pragmatism and the communist ideology. Therefore it is still possible that the policy toward the private economy may continue to be somewhat ambiguous and wavering in the foreseeable future. Even the Party's 1993 decision on further reforms still insists that the public ownership should remain the "mainstay" of the economy.[40] The 89-year-old patriarch leader Deng Xiaoping played a pivotal role in bringing in the first surge of economic reform in the 1990s. What would happen after Deng? Will the post-Deng leaders give up the pragmatism? If there is another setback of reform as the one observed in 1989 to 1990, will the implementation of hardline economic policies toward the private sector be successful?

8.4 Prospects after Deng

The non-state sectors managed to take off in the 1980s despite the unstable institutional environment. In the past two years, the Chinese government has shown stronger resolution to continue the market-oriented reform and clean up the corruptions in its organization. The leadership is likely to be continuously preoccupied with pragmatic considerations of the pressures of unemployment, the need to sustain economic growth, and government budget difficulties. With these considerations, the central and local authorities are obliged to maintain and develop the pragmatic policies developed in the 1980s.

The factors that helped ending the 1989-90 setback of reform will remain in China's economy in the years after Deng. Recently the central government has embarked on a major tax reform aiming to raise the central government's share of tax revenue from the 1993 level of 38 percent to 60 percent.[41] This reform, however, is not likely to be an easy job. It does not aim to fundamentally re-centralize local governments' decision making power and to kill the incentives for local governments to accumulate financial power. The legal protection of the private business and private property has become more effective since the new surge of reform in the 1990s. The bureaucratic corruption is still rife. These factors make any possible future setback unlikely to succeed.

It is important to note that the recent policy changes in China indicate the tendency of the central government to switch from a role akin to "followership" in the 1980s to a more active leadership in further reforms into the 1990s. The Party's 1993 decision on reform, with 50 separate articles, covers major areas of reform that were thought to be essential to build a sound base for such an economic system. These reforms, if implemented, will make China a better-ordered market economy, in which the private business has a more favorable environment to grow.

Given this background, we may conclude that China's private sector will have more friendly institutional environment than it had in the 1980s. Therefore, the momentum of the non-state-sector growth will continue.

During the 1980s, the ownership structure of Chinese economy underwent great changes. The sate-owned sector's share of total industry output value slid from near 80 percent in 1980 to about 50 percent in 1990.[42] The share of township and village enterprises in the industrial total output value increased from 14 percent to 25 percent.[43] If the trends in the 1980s continue, by the year 2000, the state sector will account only about one third of the total industrial output. The private and other non-state sectors will definitely play a more important role in China's future development.

Then what could go wrong in future? This book has shown that the growth of the private sector or entrepreneurial activity alone does not guarantee economic growth and improvement of social welfare. The welfare effects of a release of entrepreneurial energy are sensitive to institutional settings of the economic system. Is the growth of China's private sector heading to more productive uses, less productive uses, or unproductive uses of entrepreneurial resources in the coming years?

First, the uncertainty of business environment may pose a problem for future growth of entrepreneurship. As shown earlier, in the expectation for an uncertain market environment, the entrepreneurs in the 1980s tended to do their business in a myopic way by holding back important investment in capital goods, technology, goodwill and reputation. This myopic behavior might tar the image of private businesses and invite social hostility toward entrepreneurs. In the coming years, the uncertainty of business environment may not only arise from wavering official policies toward the private sector, but may also come from political instability in the post-Deng era and the deteriorating public services and law enforcement due to rampant bureaucratic corruption. Therefore, the future development of entrepreneurship depends on the robustness of the government's commitment to a market-friendly development strategy,[44] the effective public service, and the security of private property right.

The social cynicism toward law and order may also cause problems for future development of China's private sector. In Chapter 6, we have shown that private entrepreneurs played an important role in pioneering a series of institutional innovations. The reform in the 1980s was a mixture of official elite reformers' initiative and private entrepreneurs' spontaneous action to break institutional barriers. Many policy adjustments were taken to accommodate the prevailing *fait accompli* practiced by private entrepreneurs. There were some negative side-effects associated with such process.

Apart from the social costs involved in the collision between private entrepreneurs' activities and the existing institutions, the government's "followership" in these bottom-up reforms has encouraged the social cynicism toward law and order. This could become a serious barrier to the development of a better-functioning market mechanism in China. This cynicism has already made Chinese entrepreneurs less regard for the legitimacy of their actions.

In Chapter 7 we have noted that China's transitional economic system has provided plenty of opportunities for rent-seeking activities. The uncertain business environment and the widespread social cynicism have made Chinese entrepreneurs more likely to engage in rent-seeking business. According to a recent study by Murphy, Shleifer, and Vishny, rent-seeking activities exhibit very natural increasing returns:[45] First, rent-seeking system usually has a fixed cost to set up. Once set up, consequent rent-seeking becomes less costly. Second, offense creates a demand for defense. Rent-seeking is thus self-generating. Third, illicit rent-seekers have a "strength in numbers." The more people engaging, the less likely one can be caught and punished. Forth, an increase in rent-seeking activity may make rent-seeking more attractive relative to productive activity. Badly-maintained law and order thus lead to poorly protected property rights, encourage growth of rent-seeking, and kill the chance of real economic growth.

These arguments may shed light to our prospects for China's private sector and growth of entrepreneurship. If a well-ordered market economic system develops, the growth of Chinese entrepreneurship will certainly be more productive, presenting a blessing to China and the world. If, however, the Chinese government continues to be rotten with corruption it will become increasingly impotent in maintaining law and order in a society with widespread cynicism. Then property right will remain ill-defined and poorly-protected, increasing the uncertainty of business environment for productive entrepreneurship. Consequently, the unproductive use of Chinese entrepreneurial talents in rent-seeking activities will become increasingly lucrative relative to productive activities. The rampant rent-seeking will waste a substantial part of society's entrepreneurial resources. Therefore, without effectively-maintained law and order, China's transitional economy is not likely to mature into a well-ordered market economy. The widespread bureaucratic corruption has made this concern more real and serious.

Many reports of lax law enforcement and rising crimes in China have surfaced in the recent years. Organized crimes such as drug trafficking and shipment of illegal migrants to other countries have been on the rise. Tax evasion is rife.[46] More than half of the real estate developers in 1992-93 did not run any real projects but participated in speculative transactions.[47] Forgers flooded market with fake currencies.[48] Even foreign investors have taken advantage of the weakness of China's system to make money in infamous and unproductive ways.[49]

In the fifteen years after China started economic reform, the Chinese economy achieved a nine percent average annual growth rate and nearly quadrupled its GNP. However, economic crimes have grown at an even faster pace. In the 1980s, the number of cases of economic crimes accepted by procuratorial organs increased nine times at an average annual growth rate of 24.57 percent.[50] The number of crimes that were not caught could have been much larger. If the growth of unproductive activity continues to surpass the growth of productive entrepreneurship, will China's economy and its private sector in particular be able to maintain the past momentum of growth to the next century? Will China become the next "tiger" of outstanding economic growth in East Asia or another hotbed of international organized crimes in the next century?

NOTES

1. *Zhongguo Tongji Nianjian* (Statistical Yearbook of China), 1993.

2. Rohwer, Jim, "China, the Titan Stirs," *Economist* [UK], 28 November, 1992.

3. *Strait Times* [Singapore], 21 May, 1993, p. 1.

4. See Rohwer, Jim, loc. cit.

5. *Zhongguo Gongchandang Di14ci Quanguo Daibiao Daui Wenjian Huibian (Documents of the Fourteenth National Congress of CPC),* Shanghai: Jiefang Ribao Press, 1992.

6. *Renmin Ribao (People's Daily),* 17 November, 1993.

7. Ibid.

8. "Groping for planted stones while crossing a river" was an analog of reform strategy suggested by Deng. See Section 6.3 for more detail discussions.

9. *New York Times*, 8 Nov. 1989, p. 3.

10. *Renmin Ribao (People's Daily),* 27 Feb. 1990, p. 3.

11. *Zhongyang Ribao (Central Daily News),* [Taipei, Taiwan], 6 Nov. 1990, p. 4.

12. *Renmin Ribao (People's Daily),* 11 May 1990, p. 1.

13. Yearbook Editorial Board, *Yearbook on Chinese Communism* (1990), p. VII:46.

14. *China Daily* [Beijing, China], 10 Oct. 1990.

15. *Zhongyang Ribao (Central Daily News),* 24 April 1991, p. 4.

16. In November 1989, the Party's Central Committee passed "The Resolution on Further Retrenchment and Deepening of Economic Reform" to restrict the business scope of township and village enterprises, to improve taxation on the private sector and rural industries, and to crackdown on economic crimes. [*Renmin Ribao (People's Daily)*, 17 Jan. 1990, p. 1.]

17. *Renmin Ribao (People's Daily)*, 18 April 1990, p. 3.

18. *Renmin Ribao (People's Daily)*, 18 Jan. 1991, p. 1.

19. *Zhongguo Tongji Nianjian* (Statistical Yearbook of China), 1993.

20. *Zhongguo Zhi Chun (China Spring)*, No. 83 (April 1990), pp. 26-27; *Zhongyang Ribao (Centraly Daily News)*, 23 Oct. 1990, p. 4.

21. *Zhongyang Ribao (Central Daily News)*, 28 Sept. 1990, p. 4.

22. "The CPC Central Committee's Proposal for Drawing Up the Ten Year Plan of National Social and Economic Development and the Eighth Five-year Plan," ("The CPC Proposal" hereafter), *Renmin Ribao (People's Daily)*, 29 Jan. 1991, p. 3.

23. *Renmin Ribao (People's Daily)*, 19 May 1990, p. 3; 13 June 1990, p. 3; 25 June 1990, p. 3; 31 July 1990, p. 3; 23 Nov. 1990, p. 3.

24. *Renmin Ribao (People's Daily)*, 15 June 1991, p. 3.

25. *Renmin Ribao (People's Daily)*, 31 May 1990, p. 3.

26. *Renmin Ribao (People's Daily)*, 11 March 1991, p. 1.

27. Calculated according to *Zhongguo Tongji Nianjian* (Statistical Yearbook of China) 1993, Table 4-13, p. 110.

28. *Renmin Ribao (People's Daily)*, 19 Feb. 1991, p. 1. The Minister predicted earlier that the total increase of labor force in the period from 1991 to 1995 would be 36 million. [*People's Daily*, 12 December 1990, p. 3.]

29. *Zhongyang Ribao (Central Daily News)*, 23 December 1990, p. 4.

30. *Renmin Ribao (People's Daily)*, 27 March 1990, p. 3.

31. *Renmin Ribao (People's Daily)*, 19 Feb. 1991, p. 1, 26 Nov. 1991, p. 1.

32. The figure, which was based on currency exchange rate, tends to underestimate China's physical output since China's currency has devalued over the past decade. [See Rohwer, op. cit.]

33. Calculated according to the "Statistical Communique on the National Economic and Social Development During the Seventh Five-Year Plan Period (1985-90)," *Renmin Ribao (People's Daily)*, 14 March, 1991, p. 3.

34. See the Fourth Conference of the Seventh National People's Congress, "*Zhonghua Renmin Gongheguo Guominjingji he Shehui Fazhuan Shi Nian Guihua he Diba ge Wu Nian Jihua Gangyao* (The Guidelines for the Ten Year Plan of National Social and Economic Development and the Eighth Five-year Plan of the PRC)," *Renmin Ribao (People's Daily)*, 16 April 1991, pp. 1-4.

35. *Renmin Ribao (People's Daily)*, 21 Feb. 1991, p. 1.

36. *Renmin Ribao (People's Daily)*, 26 Oct. 1989, p. 3; 22 Jan. 1991, p. 1; 26 Nov. 1991, p. 1.

37. Wang Binqian (China's Minister of the State Budget Department)'s reports on state budget, 1986 to 1991, *Renmin Ribao (People's Daily)*, 14 April 1987, 8 April 1989, 10 April 1990, 12 April 1991, *Almanac of China's Economy* (1988), p. I 52-57.

38. National Statistic Bureau, "Chengxiao, Wenti, Qishi" ("Success, Problems, and Insights"), *Renmin Ribao (People's Daily)*, 25 Nov. 1991, p. 3.

39. Reuter, *Strait Times* [Singapore], 25 November, 1993, p. 8.

40. *Renmin Ribao (People's Daily)*, 17 November, 1993.

41. Reuter, *Strait Times*, 2 December, 1993, p. 40.

42. See Figure 6.1.

43. *Renmin Ribao (People's Daily)*, 22 Jan. 1991, p. 1.

44. See World Bank's *World Development Report 1991*, Washington, D.C.: Word Bank, 1991, for a detailed discussion of the market-friendly strategy.

45. Murphy, K. M., A. Shleifer, and R. W. Vishny, 1993, op. cit.

46. Reuter, AFP, *Strait Times,* 29 November, 1993, p. 6.

47. *Lianhe Zaobao (United Morning News)* [Singapore], 28 November, 1993, p. 18.

48. *Strait Times,* 29 November, 1993, p. 35.

49. Foreign investors use the privileges of foreign-invested companies to cheat the Chinese government for money in a variety of ways. Some even engage in illegal businesses such as running brothels and casinos with the cooperation of corrupt officials. [*Lianhe Zaobao (United Morning News)*, 16 May, 1993, p. 2.] Some foreign-invested companies import technojunk from industrialized countries with no concerns of environmental hazard they have brought to China.[*Strait Times*, 19 November, 1993, p. 20.]

50. *Zhongguo Jiancha Nianjian (Procuratorial Yearbook of China)*, 1091. p. 342, p. 361.

BIBLIOGRAPHY

Alm, James, "The Welfare Cost of the Underground Economy," *Economic Inquiry*, Vol. 23, no. 2, 1985, pp. 243-263.

Almanac Editorial Board, *Zhongguo Jingji Nianjian* (Almanac of China's Economy), Beijing: Publisher of Beijing Journal of Economic Management, annually published since 1981.

Almanac Editorial Board, *Almanac of China's Commerce*, Beijing: Press of Almanac of China's Commerce, annually.

Baumol, William J., "Entrepreneurship: Productive, Unproductive, and Destructive," *Journal of Political Economy*. Vol.98, no.5, pt I, 1990, pp. 893-921.

Baumol, William J., "Toward Operational Models of Entrepreneurship," in *Entrepreneurship*, J. Ronen ed. Lexington, MA: Lexington Books, 1983, pp. 28-48.

Baumol, William J., "Entrepreneurship in Economic Theory," *American Economic Review*, Vol. 58, no. 2, 1968, pp. 64-71.

Bentham, Jeremy, *Jeremy Bentham's Economic Writings*, John Bowring ed., New York: Russell & Russell, 1952.

Bhagwati, J. N., "Directly Unproductive, Profit-seeking (DUP) Activities," *Journal of Political Economy*, Vol.90, no.5, 1982, pp. 988-1002.

Blejer, M. I. and G. Szapary, "The Changing Role of Macro-economic Policies in China," *Financial Development*, Vol. 27, no. 2, 1990, pp. 32-35.

Bromley, Daniel W., "Institutional Change and Economic Efficiency," *Journal of Economic Issues,* Vol.23, no.3, Sept. 1989, pp. 735-759.

Buchanan, J. M., R.D. Tollison and G. Tullock ed., *Toward a Theory of the Rent-Seeking Society,* U.S.A.: Texas A & M University Press, 1980.

Buchanan, J. M., "Rent Seeking and Profit Seeking," in J. M. Buchanan, R. D. Tollison, G. Tullock, ed. 1980, pp. 3-15.

Cantillon, R., *Essai sur la nature dela commerce en général,* H. Higgs ed., London: Macmillan, 1931 (1755).

Casson, Mark, *The Entrepreneur: An Economic Theory,* Totowa, New Jersey: Barnes & Noble Books, 1982.

Chang, David Wen-wei, *China Under Deng Xiaoping,* New York: St. Martin's Press, 1988.

Cheng, Chu-yuan, *China's Economic Development: Growth and Structural Change,* Boulder, Colorado: Westview Press, 1982.

China Statistical Bureau, *Zhongguo Tongji Nianjian* (Statistical Yearbook of China), Beijing: China Statistical Press, annually published since 1981.

China Statistical Bureau, *China Trade and Price Statistics,* New York: Praeger Publishers, 1988.

China Statistical Bureau, *China Statistical Abstracts,* New York: Praeger Publishers, 1988, 1989, 1990.

Chinese Academy of Social Sciences, *Zhongguo Zibenzhuyi Gongshangye de Shehuizhuyi Gaizao* (Socialist Transformation of Capitalist Industry and Commerce in China), Beijing: People's Press, 1978.

Clark, John B.,"Insurance and Business Profits," *Quarterly Journal of Economics,* Vol. 7, 1892, pp. 45-54.

Clark, John B., *Essentials of Economic Theory*, New York: Macmillan, 1907.

Cole, A. H., "An Approach to the Study of Entrepreneurship," *Journal of Economic History*, supp. 6, 1946, pp. 1-15.

Diamond, D., "Financial Intermediation and Delegated Monitoring," *Review of Economic Studies*, Vol.51, July 1984, pp. 393-414.

Donnithorne, Audrey, *China's Economic System*, London: Allen and Unwin, 1967.

Donnithorne, Audrey, "China's Cellular Economy: Some Economic Trends since the Cultural Revolution," *China Quarterly*, Vol. 52, 1972, pp. 605-612.

Dong Furen, "*Jingji Jizhi he Suoyouzhi de Gaige*"("The Reform of Economic Mechanism and Ownership"), *Jingji Yanjiu* (Economic Research), No. 7, 1988, p. 27.

Fairbairn, Te'o I.J., *Island Entrepreneurs*, Honolulu, Hawaii: The East-West Center Books, 1988.

Fisher, F., "The Social Costs of Monopoly and Regulations: Posner Reconsidered," *Journal of Political Economy*, Vol. 93, 1985, pp. 410-416.

Fung, K. K., "Surplus Seeking and Rent Seeking Through Back-Door Deals in Mainland China," *American Journal of Economics and Sociology*, Vol. 46, no. 3, 1987, pp. 299-317.

Gartner, William B., "'Who is an Entrepreneur?' Is the Wrong Question," *Entrepreneurship Theory and Practice*, 1988, Spring issue.

Gifford, S. E. and C. A. Wilson, "A Model of Optimal Inspection and Repair of an Endogenous Number of Projects," C.V. Starr working paper #90-06, New York University, 1990.

Griffin, K. ed., *Institutional Reform and Economic Development in the Chinese Countryside*, New York: M.E. Sharpe, Armonk, 1984.

Grossman, S. and O. Hart, "The Cost And Benefits of Ownership: A Theory of Vertical And Lateral Integration," *Journal of Political Economy*, Vol.94, 1986, pp. 691-719.

Harding, Harry, *China's Second Revolution: Reform after Mao*, Washington, D.C.: The Brookings Institution, 1987.

Hayek, F. A., "Economics and Knowledge," *Economica* (N.S.), Vol.4, 1937, pp. 33-54; *Individualism and Economic Order*, London: Routledge and Kegan Paul, 1959.

Hayek, F. A., *The Constitution of Liberty*, Chicago: University of Chicago Press, 1960.

Hua Sheng et al., "Ten Year in China's Reform: Looking back, reflection, and prospect," *Jingji Yanjiu (Economic Research)*, no. 9, Sept. 1988, pp. 13-37.

Hebert, R. F. and A. N. Link, *The Entrepreneurship: Mainstream Views and Radical Critiques*. New York: Praeger Publishers, CBS Educational and Professional Publishing, 1982, pp. 107-110.

Hillman, A. and E. Katz, "Hierarchical Structure and the Social Cost of Bribes and Transfers," *Journal of Public Economics*. Vol. 34, 1987, pp. 129-142.

Holmstrom, B. and P. Milgrom, "Multi-Task Principal/Agent Analysis: Incentive Contracts, Asset Ownership and Job Design," Working Paper #45, Series D, Yale School of Organization and Management, 1990.

Hughes, Jonathan R.T., "Entrepreneurship," *Dictionary of Economic History*, Boston: Little Brown, 1980.

Jefferies, Ian, *A Guide to the Socialist Economies*, London and New York: Routledge, 1990.

Joint Economic Committee, *Chinese Economy Post Mao: a Compendium of Papers*, Washington, D.C.: US Government Printing Office, 1978.

Joint Economic Committee, *China's Economic Dilemmas in the 1990s: the Problems of Reforms, Modernization, and Interdependence,* Washington, D.C.: US Government Printing Office, 1991.

Kantorovich, L.V., *The Best Use of Economic Resources,* Cambridge: Harvard University Press, 1965.

Kihlstrom, R. E. and J. Laffont, "A General Equilibrium Entrepreneurial Theory of Firm Formation Based on Risk Aversion," *Journal of Political Economy,* Vol.87, no.4, 1979, pp. 719-748.

Kilby, P., *Entrepreneurship and Economic Development,* New York: Free Press, 1971.

Kirzner, I. M., *Perception, Opportunity, and Profit,* Chicago: The University of Chicago Press, 1979.

Knight, F. W., *Risk, Uncertainty and Profit,* New York: Harper and Row, 1965(1921).

Kornai, János, "The Affinity Between Ownership Forms and Coordination Mechanisms: The Common Experience of Reform in Socialist Countries," *Journal of Economic Perspectives,* Vol. 4, no. 3, 1990, pp. 131-147.

Kornai, János, "The Hungarian Reform Process: Vision, Hopes, and Reality," *Journal of Economic Literature,* Vol 24, Dec. 1986, pp. 1687-1737.

Kornai, János, *Contradictions and Dilemmas,* Cambridge: First MIT Press edition, 1986

Kraus, Willy, *Economic Development and Social Change in the People's Republic of China.* New York: Springer-Verlag, 1982.

Kraus, Willy, *Private Business in China,* Honolulu, Hawaii: University of Hawaii Press, 1991, pp.180-184.

Lardy, Nicholas R. and Kenneth Lieberthal ed., *Chen Yun's Strategy for China's Development—— a Non-Maoist Alternative*, New York: M.E. Sharpe, Inc., 1983.

Lardy, N., "Economic Planning in the People's Republic of China: Central-Provincial Fiscal Relations," U.S. Congress, Joint Economic Committee, *China: A Reassessment of the Economy*, Washington, D.C.: Joint Committee Print, 1975.

Leibenstein, Harvey, "Entrepreneurship and Development," *American Economic Review*, Vol.52, no.2, 1968, pp. 72-83.

Leff, N. H., "Entrepreneurship and Economic Development: the Problem Revisited," *Journal of Economic Literature*, Vol. 17, 1979, pp. 46-64.

Levine, H.S., "On the Nature and Location of Entrepreneurial Activity in Centrally Planned Economies: The Soviet Case" in *Entrepreneurship*, Joshua Ronen ed., Lexington, MA: Lexington Books, 1983, pp. 235-267.

Libecap, G. ed. *Advances in the Study of Entrepreneurship, Innovation, and Economic Growth*, Vol. 1-2. Greenwood, CT: JAI Press, 1987-88.

Liu Suinian and Wu Qungan ed., *China's Socialist Economy—— An Outline History (1949-1984)*, Beijing, China: Beijing Review, 1986.

Magee, Stephen P., William R. Brock, and Leslie Young, *Black Hole Tariffs and the Endogenous Policy Theory*, Cambridge: Cambridge University Press, 1989.

Mao Zedong, *Selected Works of Mao Zedong*, 5 vols, Beijing, China: Foreign Language Press, 1965-77.

Marrese, Michael, "Entrepreneurship, Liberalization, and Social Tension," *Jahrbuch der Wirtshaft Osteuropas* Vol.14, no.1, 1990, pp. 1-15.

Mason, Edward S., "Monopolistic Competition and the Growth Process in Less Developed Countries: Chamberlin and the Schumpeterian

Dimension," in *Monopolistic Competition Theory: Studies in Impact,* R.E. Kuenne ed. New York: Wiley, 1967, pp. 77-104.

Mises, L. von, *Human Action: A Treatise of Economics,* New Haven, Conn.: Yale University Press, 1949.

Mo Zhen, "Tighten Control over Big Labor-Hiring Households in Rural Areas," *Chinese Economic Studies,* Vol. 21 no.2, 1987, pp. 90-95.

Murphy, Kevin M., Andrei Shleifer, and Robert W. Vishny, "The Allocation of Talent: Implications for Growth," *The Quarterly Journal of Economics,* Vol.106, May 1991, pp. 503-530.

Murphy, K. M., A. Shleifer, and R. W. Vishny, "Why is Rent-Seeking So Costly to Growth?" *AEA Papers and Proceedings,* May 1993, pp. 409-414.

Panico, Joseph A., *Queuing Theory: a Study of Waiting Lines for Business, Economics, and Science,* Englewood Cliffs, New Jersey: Prentice-Hall Inc., 1969.

Perkins, Dwight H., "Reforming China's Economic System," *Journal of Economic Literature,* Vol. 26, June 1988, pp. 601-645.

Posner, R., "The Social Costs of Monopoly and Regulation," *Journal of Political Economy,* Vol. 83, 1975, pp. 807-827.

Prybyla, Jan S., *The Political Economy of Communist China,* Scranton, Pennsylvania: International Textbook Company, 1970.

Prybyla, Jan S., *Reform in China and Other Socialist Economies,* Lanham, Maryland: University Press of America.

Radner, R. and M. Rothschild, "On Allocation of Effort," *Journal of Economic Theory.* no. 10, 1975, pp. 358-376.

Rohwer, Jim, "China, the Titan Stirs," *Economist* [UK], 28 November, 1992.

Ronen, Joshua ed., *Entrepreneurship*, Lexington, MA: Lexington Books.

Rosen, Stanley, "The Private Economy," *Chinese Economic Studies*, Vol. XXI, No.1 (1987), pp. 3-9.

Sanchez, N. and A. R. Waters, "Controlling Corruption in Africa and Latin America," in *The Economics of Property Rights*, E. G. Furuboton and S. Pejovich ed., Cambridge, Mass.: Ballinger Publishing Company, 1974, pp. 279-295.

Schmöller, G., *The Mercantile System*, New York: Smith, 1891

Schultz, Theodore W., "The Value of the Ability to Deal With Disequilibria," *Journal of Economic Literature*, Vol.13, 1975, pp. 827-46.

Schumpeter, J.A., *Capitalism, Socialism and Democracy*, New York: Harper and Row, 1942.

Shi Xiaomin and Liu Jirui, "Review on 'Ten Years in China's Reform'," *Jingji Yanjiu (Economic Research)*, no. 2, 1989, pp. 11-33.

Smith, Adam, *The Wealth of Nations*, New York: Random House, Modern Library Edition, 1937 [1776].

Soto, Hernando de, *The Other Path: the Invisible Revolution in the Third World*, London: I. B. Tauris, 1989.

State Statistical Bureau of The People's Republic of China (PRC), *Ten Great Years*, Beijing: Foreign Language Press, 1960.

Statistical Bureau of the People's Republic of China, *China Statistical Abstract*, New York: Praeger Publishers, annually.

Statistical Bureau of the People's Republic of China, *Statistical Yearbook of China*, Beijing: China Statistical Press, annually.

Thünen, J.M. von. *Isolated State*, Peter Hall ed., Oxford: Pergaman, 1966.

Tirole, J., *The Theory of Industrial Organization*, Cambridge, MA.: The MIT Press, 1988, pp. 76-77.

Walder, Andrew G. "Local Bargaining Relationships and Urban Industrial Finance," in *Bureaucracy, Politics, and Decision Making in Post-Mao China*, K. Lieberthal and D. Lampton ed., Berkeley, California: University of California Press, 1992.

Weber, Max, *The Protestant Ethic and the Spirit of Capitalism*, translated by T. Parsons, New York: Scribner's, 1930.

Wellisz, S. and R. Findlay, "Central Planning and the 'Second Economy' in Soviet-Type Systems," *The Economic Journal*, Vol. 96, Sept.1986, pp. 646-658.

Wilken, P.H., *Entrepreneurship: a Comparative and Historical Study*, Norwood, NJ: Ables Publishing Corporation, 1979.

Winter, S. G. "The Case for 'Mechanistic' Decision Making," *Organizational Strategy and Change*, J. M. Pennings et al ed. San Francisco: Jossey-Bass Publishers, 1985, pp. 99-113.

Woo, Henry K. H., *Effective Reform in China: an Agenda*, New York: Praeger Publishers, 1991.

Wu Jinglian and Zhao Renwei, "The Dual Pricing System in China's Industry," *Journal of Comparative Economics*, No. 11, 1987, pp. 309-318.
Wu Jinglian and Bruce Reynolds, "Choosing a Strategy for China's Economic Reform," paper presented at the annual meetings of the American Economic Association, Chicago, December 1987.

Xie Baogui, "The Function of the Chinese Procuratorial Organ in the Combat against Corruption," *Asian Journal of Public Administration*, Vol. 10, no. 1, Jun 1988, pp. 73-75.

Xu Dixin, *Zhongguo Guodu Shiqi Guomin Jingji Fenxi* (An Analysis on China's National Economy in the Transformation Period: 1946-57). Beijing, China: People's Press, 1962.

Xue Muqiao, Su Xing, and Lin Zili, *Zhongguo Guomin Jingji de Shehui Zhuyi Gaizao* (The Socialist Transformation of China's National Economy), Beijing, China: People's Press, 1964.

Xue Muqiao, *Zhongguo Shehuizhuyi Jingji Wenti Yanjiu* (Study of China's Socialist Economic Problems), Beijing: People's Press, 1979.

Xue Muqiao, *"Woguo Shengchan Ziliao Suoyouzhi de Yanbian"* (The Evolution of the Ownership of Production Means in China), *Jingji Yanjiu* (Economic Research) [Beijing, China], No. 2, 1982, pp. 18-19.

Yang Jianbai, *Zhonghua Renmin Gongheguo Guomin Jingji Huifu he Fazhan de Chengjiu* (The Success of Rehabilitating and Developing the National Economy in the P.R. China). Beijing, China: Statistical Press, 1956.

Yearbook Editorial Board, *Zhong Gong Nianjian (Yearbook on Chinese Communism) 1989*, Taipei, Taiwan: The Institute for the Study of Chinese Communist Problems, annually.

Zhang Renze and Mo-yin S. Tam, "Changes in Income Distributions in China in the Process of Economic Reform in the 1980s: a Welfare Approach," Working paper, University of Illinois at Chicago, 1990.

Zhu Qingfang, "On the Evolution and Changes of the Individual Economy," *Chinese Economic Studies*, Vol. 21, no.2, Winter 1987-88, pp. 100-176.

Zhongguo Jiancha Nianjian (Procuratorial Yearbook of China), Beijing: China Procuratorial Press, annually.

INDEX